Critical acclaim for Darling Judi:

'*Darling Judi* is devoid of sentimentality. It consists of intimate snapshots, full of joy and irreverence, and studied attempts to capture her brilliance ... One thing that all the contributors emphasise is that Dame Judi's greatness as an actress is also her greatness as a person' Michael Arditti, *Daily Mail*

'A must-read for theatre buffs' Roger Lewis, *Sunday Express*

'Contains ... a great many amusing and affectionate anecdotes ... [Dench] emerges as a mercurial figure, with a larky sense of humour ... the book offers some arresting descriptions of her acting style' *The Times*

'Characteristically thorough and painstaking ... about as close to her secret soul as we shall get in a well-guarded private lifetime' Sheridan Morley, *Sunday Times*

'An intriguing life of a witty, intelligent and intriguing actress' Maeve Brown, *Irish Independent* (Dublin)

'Respect, love, admiration, adoration, even adulation, enough to turn someone's head if they were less realistic – yet a well-rounded personality emerges; a giggler, a practical joker, full of mischief as well as compassionate and considerate ... This is a book which you could read in one sitting, but it is even better if you dip into it from time to time. Miller has compiled an engaging portrait and provided us with insights into this great actor' *The Press* (Christchurch, New Zealand)

'Amusing and enlightening reminiscences' *Theatregoer*

The editor, John Miller, is the author – in addition to his life of Judi Dench – of biographies of Ralph Richardson and Peter Ustinov. He also collaborated with John Gielgud on *An Actor and His Time* and *Acting Shakespeare*, and with John Mills on his 1980 updated memoir *Up in the Clouds, Gentlemen Please.*

Darling Judi

A celebration of
JUDI DENCH

Introduced and edited by
John Miller

ORION

An Orion paperback

First published in Great Britain in 2004
by Weidenfeld & Nicolson
This paperback edition published in 2005
by Orion Books Ltd,
Orion House, 5 Upper St Martin's Lane,
London WC2H 9EA

Revised edition

1 3 5 7 9 10 8 6 4 2

A CIP catalogue record for this book is
available from the British Library.

ISBN 0 75286 462 9

Typeset in Great Britain by
Butler and Tanner Ltd, Frome and London

Printed and bound in Great Britain by
Clays Ltd, St Ives plc

www.orionbooks.co.uk

To a great actress and a very special friend.

Contents

Contents

List of Illustrations

One of the youngest members of the Old Vic Company, 1957[1].

Anya in *The Cherry Orchard*, with John Gielgud as Gaev. Royal Shakespeare Company, 1961[2].

Titania in *A Midsummer Night's Dream*, with Ian Richardson as Oberon. Royal Shakespeare Company, 1962[3].

Isabella in *Measure for Measure*. Royal Shakespeare Company, 1962[4].

Viola in *Twelfth Night*. Royal Shakespeare Company, 1969[3].

Backstage during *London Assurance*. Royal Shakespeare Company, 1972[2].

With Finty at BAFTA, 2001[5].

Adriana in *The Comedy of Errors*, with Michael Williams as one of the Dromio twins. Royal Shakespeare Company, 1976[3].

Beatrice in *Much Ado About Nothing*, with Donald Sinden as Benedick. Royal Shakespeare Company, 1976[6].

With Richard Pasco and Michael Williams at the Royal Shakespeare Company[1].

Laura in *A Fine Romance*, with Michael Williams as Mike. London Weekend Television, 1980[5].

Jean in *As Time Goes By*, with Geoffrey Palmer as Lionel. BBC, 1992–2002[5].

Juno in *Juno and the Paycock*, with Dearbhla Molloy as Mary Boyle. Royal Shakespeare Company, Aldwych, 1980[7].

Lady Bracknell in *The Importance of Being Earnest*. National Theatre, 1982[8].

Barbara in *Pack of Lies*, with Michael Williams as Bob. Lyric Theatre, 1983[7].

Carrie Pooter in *Mr and Mrs Nobody*, with Michael Williams as Charles Pooter. Garrick Theatre, 1986[7].

Mother Courage. Royal Shakespeare Company, 1984[9].

Cleopatra, with Anthony Hopkins as Antony. National Theatre, 1987[10].

Desirée in *A Little Night Music*: backstage with Laurence Guittard (Fredrik). National Theatre, 1995[12].

Researching *Entertaining Strangers*, with Tim Pigott-Smith and the company. National Theatre, 1987[11].

Filumena, with Michael Pennington as Domenico. Piccadilly, 1998[13].

Making-up for Esmé in *Amy's View.* National Theatre, 1999[2].

With Billy Connolly, who played John Brown to her Queen Victoria in *Mrs Brown*, 1996[5].

Winning the Academy Award for *Shakespeare in Love*, 1999[5].

Iris Murdoch in *Iris*, with Jim Broadbent as John Bayley. Miramax Films, 2001[5].

The Countess Rossillion in *All's Well That Ends Well.* Royal Shakespeare Company, 2003[14].

Dame Judi Dench by Alessandro Raho, 2005[15].

The editor and publishers are grateful to Judi Dench, and to many of the contributors to the book for their assistance in supplying photographs.

[1] Barbara Leigh-Hunt
[2] John Timbers
[3] Joe Cocks Studio Collection, Shakespeare Birthplace Trust
[4] Gordon Goode, Shakespeare Birthplace Trust
[5] Rex Features Ltd
[6] Reg Wilson, Royal Shakespeare Company
[7] Donald Cooper
[8] Zoë Dominic
[9] Nobby Clark
[10] John Haynes

List of Illustrations

Acknowledgements

I would like to express my particular thanks to all my fellow-contributors to this book, who responded with such enthusiasm and alacrity to the invitation to write about someone so special to all of us. I know how busy each one of them is, and that the task entailed quite a bit of burning the midnight oil to meet the deadline. In addition to confiding some very personal reminiscences, they also searched for a number of the pictures, which trace the development of Judi Dench's career from the Old Vic in 1957 to the RSC in 2004. The Note on the Contributors on page 201 explains their particular connection with her.

I am very grateful to Ion Trewin for asking me to oversee this celebratory volume, and for all his most helpful suggestions; and to his assistant, Anna Hervé, for her prompt response to all my requests, and especially for her assistance with the picture research. My thanks also to John Timbers for creating the cover picture, and for capturing over the years some significant moments in the life of Judi Dench.

Lastly, and most importantly, I must, of course, thank the subject herself. Because of its nature I have not consulted Judi about the contents of this book, but I could never have attempted to put it together if it had not been for her extraordinary generosity when I was writing her biography, and for her many gestures of friendship since. This gives me the chance to repay at least a little of the great debt I owe her.

John Miller
June, 2004

Fondly Familiar

JOHN MILLER

Ever since I embarked on writing the biography of Judi Dench the two questions I have most often been asked are: 'Is she really as nice as she seems?' and 'What is it that makes her such a great actress?'

The first question is much easier to answer than the second, and my response always is, 'She's even nicer, when you get to know her,' as I have been so privileged to do. In the following chapters my fellow authors without exception reveal the depth of their own affection for her but, as you will read, even those who have worked most closely with her find it as difficult as I do to pin down the inner secret of her genius.

What does, however, become very clear from the contributions to this book is that it is her qualities as a person – her ready sympathy, her alert sensitivity to the problems of others, her quick intelligence, her bubbling sense of humour, her astonishing generosity and thoughtfulness – which combine with her innate truthfulness in every part she plays to create a character that can reduce you to tears or laughter, often with just a look or a gesture, an inflection, or sometimes even just a momentary pause.

When my publisher first asked me to gather these reminiscences together to celebrate Judi's seventieth birthday in December 2004, I hesitated for more than just a moment for two reasons. Very few ladies of my acquaintance are keen to mark the end of a decade, and I wasn't at all sure that Judi would want to draw attention to this significant date either. Secondly, how many of her friends and colleagues would be willing or able to set down their feelings about her in such a book? The latter doubt was swiftly dispelled. Although two or three of them were either too heavily engaged in current acting commitments, or too diffident about their writing skills to feel they could do justice to her, everyone else who is included here agreed instantly, and couldn't wait to put on the public record their admiration of someone who is so special to all of them.

As I suspected, Judi herself was initially much less keen on such a book. Having attended her televised BAFTA Fellowship evening at the Haymarket, and also sat next to her in the Barrymore Theater in New York when she was awarded the Golden Quill by the Shakespeare Guild, I knew how praise seems to embarrass her, and how relieved she is when someone breaks the mood by sending her up. But I pointed out to her that her impending birthday was already public knowledge, and she could hardly escape it being celebrated by her many friends and admirers. Although John Gielgud had told me that he didn't want too much fuss about his being ninety ten years ago, for fear that anyone might think he had retired and consequently stop offering him work, it will be many years before Judi faces a similar dilemma.

However, to spare her blushes, and to keep this as a birthday surprise, I haven't let her see these expressions of love and admiration before they are published. I hope and believe that she will be even more touched and thrilled to read them than I was when they started tumbling through my letterbox or coming off the fax machine.

The criterion for selection was a simple one. All these actors, directors and writers have either worked with her or followed her career over a long period, from her arrival at the Old Vic in 1957 up to her most recent stage performance with the RSC in 2004. Each of them brings a different perspective to bear on her personality and her great talent, which when read together reveal both her extraordinary range and her depth of character. From Shakespeare to sitcom, in the classics and modern work, on stage and screen, Judi Dench has never ceased to surprise us with her next move, and in recent years she has gained an international following as devoted as the one she has long possessed in Britain.

I asked each of the contributors to write about Judi in as personal a way as possible, and it is time I did the same. One of the rewards of becoming her biographer has been the number of invitations to share a platform with her to talk about her work. The first time at the National Theatre in 1998 I was caught off guard by the overwhelming surge of affection for her that rolled up onto the stage, it was so palpable. I have since grown used to having to wait several minutes for the applause to fade and allow me to put my first question. The noisiest welcomes were in two very different venues. The students at the Oxford Union greeted her with a thundering, foot-stamping ovation which showed how much her appeal crossed all generations. Most recently, in April 2004, the Cheltenham Festival of Literature booked us into the huge new Centaur Arena at the Racecourse, which drew an audience of over 1,800. We were asked to concentrate exclusively on discussing Judi's Shakespearean career, but from the whistling and whooping as we walked out on-stage you might well have thought that Judi was about to perform at a pop-concert. A little surprised but not at all disconcerted, she just hissed at me out of the corner of her mouth, 'I think we'd better take a bow.'

Watching her rehearse and perform a show is even more eye-opening. In 2003 I invited her to bring *Fond and Familiar* to the Winchester Festival. This was the comic recital which John Moffatt devised at the request of Judi and Michael, and over the years she has performed it with a number of different actors. This time we managed to get Ian Richardson and Bill Nighy to accompany her, neither of whom had ever done the show before. So at the read-through at Judi's home on the Wednesday beforehand, whenever we reached one of her long monologues she skipped straight to the last verse, just to give them their next cue. She said, 'You boys need the rehearsal time much more than I do, I've done this show dozens of times.' She did the same thing at the Sunday afternoon rehearsal at the Theatre Royal, which meant that the first time the other two actors heard her big set-piece recitations was that evening, with the audience in. Naturally the latter were all watching her, but I couldn't help noticing with amusement how the two men sat there transfixed by what she did with those monologues. After the last one, Ian involuntarily responded: 'My God, how d'you follow that?!'

He and Judi had been a famous Oberon and Titania with the RSC at Stratford in 1962, and they re-created those roles for the John Gielgud Centenary Gala in April 2004, a performance described later in these pages. All I would add here is that when Judi skipped barefoot on to the stage she didn't seem a day over twenty-five, and the packed house at the Gielgud Theatre was entranced.

This was near the end of the London run of *All's Well*, during which she had often also been filming new scenes of her science-fiction movie *The Chronicles of Riddick*, so she had been fully stretched for weeks. She asked me, 'As I'm only on in the first half, I don't suppose there's any chance I could slip away at the interval?' I felt awfully mean having to reply, 'Well, Jude, we really need you all for the final curtain-call, and everyone will be expecting to see you.' My guilt was somewhat assuaged when she told me afterwards what an increasingly riotous party she had hosted in her dressing room, as everyone else came offstage after their own performances and joined her. What made that gathering so special for her was that it reunited her with so many of her former co-stars, several of whom have contributed to these printed memories.

Acting is an elusive art, and the secret of truly great acting can never be totally unlocked for such exponents as John Gielgud or Ralph Richardson, Peggy Ashcroft or Judi Dench. But there are moments when we know we are unmistakably in its presence, when the hair on the back of the neck stands on end; and there are many such moments described vividly in this book, as telling in the back of the stalls or gallery as they are to the other actors on stage. Two that stand out particularly in my memory are the despair that Judi conveyed as Lika in the last act of *The Promise* at the realisation that she had married the wrong man; and her rendering of 'Send in the clowns' in *A Little Night Music*, as a tear coursed slowly down her cheek at the end of the song.

Her tears on stage are never forced, they flow naturally from the emotional demands of the scene. Even in rehearsal for *Amy's View* I watched her cry real tears every time she exited at one point, and I couldn't help thinking that many other actresses would have saved them up for the actual performances. But she had lost herself so completely in the part that she simply couldn't help portraying the full emotional climax as David Hare had written it.

All great actors are possessed of the most perfect comic timing, and some of the most sustained and sparkling examples of Judi's were to be seen in her hugely popular television sitcoms, *A Fine Romance* and *As Time Goes By*, the first with her real husband Michael Williams, and the second with Geoffrey Palmer, whom the fans of that show persist in regarding as her actual husband. I spent a week observing the rehearsal and recording of an episode of the latter, when she would frequently say, 'I don't need this line, I can get the laugh with just a look.' When the studio audience was in, she always did too. The double-take is an effective comic instrument in the right hands, but I have often seen Judi do a triple-take, and get three laughs, each one greater than the last. Whenever we have done joint book-signings after a Platform conversation, I have soon lost count of the number of people expressing their heartfelt appreciation of the pleasure that those TV performances have given them.

This book is for all those admirers, whether they have watched her on the stage, on television or on the cinema screen or, like many of us, on all three. But above all, this is for you, Darling Judi, with our love and gratitude for all the joy you have brought us since you first stepped onto that Old Vic stage in 1957.

We all wish you A Very Happy Birthday, and many, many happy returns.

Only Playing?

BENEDICT NIGHTINGALE

Judi Dench has played several actresses in her time, among them Arkadina in Chekhov's *Seagull* and Desirée Armfeldt in Sondheim's *A Little Night Music*, but there are two that stick especially in my mind, and not merely because I saw them more recently. In each case, Dame Judi wasn't just giving her usual impeccably judged and felt-through performance: she seemed to be telling us something deeply serious about the calling that has sustained her and us since she went on the professional stage back in 1957.

Let's face it, even Peter Hall's direction couldn't persuade us that George Kaufman and Edna Ferber's comic celebration of the Barrymore dynasty, *The Royal Family*, was in urgent need of revival in the London of 2001. For all the skill of Julia Mackenzie, Harriet Walter, and Toby Stephens as a chaotic, swashbuckling Hollywood star in a Cyrano costume, it wasn't all that funny. But then Judi Dench's Fanny, the matriarch of the clan, was one of the few characters in the play not meant to be funny. She was pale, she was sick, and at the very end of the play she died; for her the stage wasn't an opportunity either to show off or to accumulate money and fame.

No, it was a vocation that demanded utter commitment and total professionalism, and clearly got them from her. To hear Dame Judi's Fanny coolly yet passionately describe preparing for a performance, or reiterate her determination to return to the boards, or tell her doubting granddaughter that her acting was 'everything: work and play and meat and drink', was to hear something unforgettable: a testimony to the power of the theatre that, you felt, flowed as much from the heart of the English dame as from the grande dame of the American stage.

The second performance came in 1997 in David Hare's *Amy's View*, in which Dame Judi played a feisty, doughty British actress who ended up losing pretty much everything: her beloved daughter, her own fiancé, her money, her house and her hopes of substantial success in the theatre. Yet there she was, sitting in her dressing room, quietly making up her face, waiting to appear in a play she thought a bit callow and pretentious yet also sincere and even 'special'. And the gravity of Dame Judi's looks and the grimly defiant set of her jaw as she prepared for her entry, and then went onstage, told us without need for more words what she and Hare believed. The theatre matters. The theatre is unique. The theatre lives.

I have to say I was much moved by what struck me as very close to a personal confession from a great actress with over forty years' experience under her belt; and yet, as I write these words, I realise that I'm in danger of getting pompous and portentous. And the paradox of Dame Judi is that, though no actor is more painstaking about her craft and art, none is less pretentious about either. Even as she exposes her soul she has, so to speak, one foot on the ground. She likes to quote Michael Benthall, who directed her Ophelia back in 1957: 'It's only a play, you know.' Partly this means that, unlike the sort of Method actor who goes into a self-absorbed rapture when he has to play a spear-carrier, Dame Judi knows that in the cosmic scheme of things the drama, like just about everything else, is transitory, ephemeral and at times a bit absurd. Partly, it reflects the innate humility of a woman whose strengths include humour, self-criticism and a refusal to be insti-tutionalised as 'great'. Partly, it's a way of reminding us and herself that the theatre is also entertainment, fun – and can often be of the earth earthy.

She's a complex, contradictory person, this Dench, and much

the same as an actress. I've seen her be poignant, larky, sombre, slatternly, loving, grave, hilarious, coarse, majestic and a score of other things. You couldn't say she has a distinct 'style', as that gloriously subtle ironist, Maggie Smith, has a style. And even Vanessa Redgrave can't match her versatility. How many other actresses could make outstanding successes of Viola and Mother Courage, Cleopatra and Beatrice, Millamant and Lady Macbeth, O'Casey's Juno and Wilde's Lady Bracknell, the raucous, vulgar Christine in Rodney Ackland's *Absolute Hell* and the grieving, lovelorn Queen Victoria of the film *Mrs Brown*, the middle-aged child who has returned to life from near-coma in Harold Pinter's *A Kind of Alaska* and the title-character in Eduardo de Filippo's *Filumena*?

Back in 1997, I had a chat with Dame Judi as she prepared to perform the last of these characters and, though she habitually agrees to appear in plays before she has read them, and did precisely that when Peter Hall offered her this particular part, her surprise at her casting was still evident. Filumena, you see, is a streetwise Neapolitan, an ex-prostitute who manipulates her long-time lover into marrying her on a 'death-bed' from which she promptly springs, restored to health and ready to do battle on behalf of the sons the poor, disoriented man never knew she had. Nobody, said Dame Judi at one point, would have dreamed of giving her such a role in a film.

'Why not?' I asked.

'It's hard to explain,' she replied, 'but in a film there's too much of me. In the theatre I can sublimate myself and my personality much more. I can fool you into thinking I'm taller or older or younger than I am. In a film you're cast because of what you look like, but in the theatre you're not. And you have the opportunity to control yourself and your audience.'

That says plenty about the limitations of that over-literal medium, the film, and that gymnasium for lively imaginations, the theatre; but it also says plenty about Dame Judi. The great actor has the power, the nerve, the assurance, the immediacy and finally the undefinable magic to bounce you into believing the barely believable and agreeing that lead is silver or silver gold. And theatrical history tells us that the great actor has often overcome what might seem physical disadvantage. The aging Kean, for instance, was small, sickly and so hoarse he sounded like 'a hackney coachman at one o'clock in the morning', yet when his Othello scuttled in a gouty hobble up to William Macready's much taller Iago and grabbed him by the throat, Kean 'seemed to swell into a stature that made Macready seem small'.

Well, Dame Judi will, I'm sure, be pleased to be reassured that at seventy and rising she's very far from the dissipated wreck that Kean became at a considerably younger age, but she is five-foot two and she does have a voice that once led her to consider putting up a notice for concerned spectators in the foyer of the Palace Theatre, where she was playing Sally Bowles in *Cabaret*: 'Miss Judi Dench does not have a cold. This is her normal speaking voice.' Yet that slight huskiness, the crack in her voice, call it what you will, has become a strength, for, in a curious way, it adds texture and depth, and sometimes pain and melancholy, to whatever character she's playing. When you hear it you know that, even if she's in a major-key role, the possibility of moving into a minor key exists.

Similarly with her height. She likes to joke about this, and, when Peter Hall asked her to play Cleopatra, she famously asked him why he wanted to cast 'a menopausal dwarf' in the role. There are, of course, occasions on which Dame Judi's lack of inches works for her. Who can forget her tiny, battling Mother Courage, finding it harder and harder to keep tugging a big, awkward cart round and round the Barbican stage? But I can't remember it working against her. Her Cleopatra did not lack magnificence or, indeed, size as she prepared for death, nor did she get the wrong kind of laughter when she described her rival Octavia as 'dull of tongue and dwarfish'. And if I had been asked to guess the height of her Filumena – not something that occurred to me as she seized my imagination in the theatre – I would have said she was a formidable, even lanky five-foot eight or so.

But the important matters are, of course, the emotions Dame Judi can command and the intelligence which, along with a clarity of diction that's becoming sadly rare even when the major classics are being performed by major companies, she brings to our stage. And from the very first she's had the ability to radiate warmth, generosity of heart and, especially, love without becoming sentimental or implausible. All right, she began her career inauspiciously, getting reviews for the Ophelia she played at the Old Vic in 1957 – 'a piece of Danish patisserie' – so grudging and, frankly, sexist they would have floored a less resilient woman. But John Neville, who played Hamlet in the same revival, thought she was 'very fine', since 'she had exactly the right quality – vulnerability'. And she went on to justify his faith not only at the Vic, where Kenneth Tynan brought his critical weight to defend Zeffirelli's unwontedly realistic production of *Romeo and Juliet* against its detractors, and praised Judi Dench's Juliet for calmness, wisdom and an encounter with John Stride's Romeo that was 'grave, awkward and extremely beautiful', but also at Neville's own Nottingham Playhouse.

This is where I myself entered the picture as her reviewer, for I briefly became the *Guardian*'s northern theatre critic and especially valued my visits to a spanking new theatre which then represented all that was fresh, hopeful and exciting in the British regions. I saw Judi Dench as a strong, moving Isabella in an updated *Measure for Measure* in 1965, and I saw her opposite Edward Woodward's Elyot as Amanda in Coward's *Private Lives* later the same year, remarking on the skill and wit with which she conveyed not only the character's egoism but the rapport between herself and her ex-husband: 'Together they successfully suggest that any honest love necessarily involves anger, frustration, jealousy and even violence.'

That airy reference to violence makes me feel uneasy now – though, when I recall Dame Judi's Cleopatra, it doesn't seem wholly misguided – but the overall point still stands. This actress isn't only uniquely effective at incarnating love in its more straightforward manifestations: Imogen, Perdita, Chekhov's Anya, and a Maria who did indeed adore Toby Belch. She's without parallel when it comes to suggesting love's intricacies and contradictions. I could cite a sweet, vital Viola, performed for the RSC at Stratford in 1969, who was wryly amused at the absurdity of wooing a rival in male disguise, yet brought a quiet intensity to the 'patience on a monument' speech and seemed almost eager to die at the hands of Richard Pasco's Orsino when he turned on her, venomously accused her of treachery and, sounding as if he meant it, threatened her with murder. I could cite her Ranevskaya in *The Cherry Orchard*, denying her love for the unworthy man she's left in Paris yet surreptitiously keeping and hiding the letter she'd just ostentatiously torn up, or her Arkadina in *The Seagull*, kittenish but cunning and so desperately afraid of losing her youth, her looks and her Trigorin that she wrestled him to the ground, lay on top of him, and began to tug off his trousers: a moment that gave extra frisson to the words with which she implored him to leave the house for Moscow: 'You will come, yes?'

But the key case was surely that Cleopatra in 1987, a fine demonstration of Dame Judi's well-known ability to skip seamlessly from mood to mood, feeling to feeling, as well as of her equally admired knack for conveying love. She was variously languorous, capricious, sad, nostalgic when she recalled her salad days, exuberant, imperious, scornful, reflective, impetuous, sullen, scarily angry, stunningly quick-witted, and inadvertently funny when the realisation that Octavia was younger than her sent her dashing in dismay, rage and panic for the exit. Typically, Dame Judi said that only once in the hundred times she played the part did she come close to getting it right; but that wasn't the view of the critics, who recognised her near-infinite variety and especially the truth and force of the love that underpinned everything.

And with love often come loss, pain, grief, melancholy: feelings that didn't only mark the last moments of her Cleopatra but have characterised many of her performances. If nobody is better at communicating relief, rapture and hard-earned delight than Dame Judi – think of her Beatrice, suddenly believing in the hostile Benedick's devotion, or her Filumena, softening and sobbing as she realises that she can at long last stop screaming inside and put aside her slum ferocity – nobody is better at expressing regret, sorrow, desolation, despair.

Here, let's not forget her Mrs Rafi in Edward Bond's *The Sea*, an upper-crust gorgon who has spent her life tyrannising others yet ends up bleak and alone, looking askance at herself and realising she has squandered her life playing arid power-games and can hope only for a loveless old age. But here let's especially remember her Desirée, the grande dame who has wryly, stubbornly, doughtily survived lovers, disappointments and a lifetime of playing Hedda Gabler in the Scandinavian provinces. When Dame Judi delivered Sondheim's 'Send in the clowns', it wasn't a sentimental dirge, still less a pretty crowd-pleaser but a carefully pondered piece of self-criticism and a deeply felt confession of personal failure. I can still remember the surprise and the applause as the National Theatre audience realised that Judi Dench had used her acting skills, including the crack in her voice, to reclaim an over-familiar song for emotional truth.

Emotional openness would, I suppose, sum up Dame Judi's core strength, but it's inadequate to explain her range. The improbable is a positive come-on for her. 'I love it when people push me and say go on, try it, go on, fall 3,000 feet and see how you feel,' she once told me. 'I like variety and risk and unsuitability. Nobody thought I could play Cleopatra, for instance, or Lady Bracknell. But I hate being bored and that's the way to avoid boredom and learn something new.'

Actually Peggy Ashcroft, Dame Judi's friend, support and mentor, begged her not to attempt Wilde's lady tyrannosaurus. But the opportunity to take a fresh look at a role that seemed to have been defined for all time by Edith Evans was too tempting. And, as often with Dame Judi, unexpected casting led to an unexpected interpretation. For one thing, she latched on to several usually unnoticed aspects of Lady Bracknell, such as the fact that she appeared to despise a husband with whom she had presumably made a socially and financially advantageous marriage, probably in her own salad days. So her Bracknell seemed younger than usual and rather too attracted to her handsome nephew, Algy.

Gradually Lady Bracknell the mythic monster evolved into Lady Bracknell the all-too-human snob and serenely avaricious bully. Even the bons mots were more real than usual, for this woman took conscious pride in uttering them and not a little satisfaction in the power over others they gave her. And when she came to the moment we were all waiting for, 'A hand-bag?', the words didn't emerge, Evans-style, as a gigantic upper-crust gasp of affronted horror. Dame Judi slowly removed her spectacles, whispered 'A hand-bag?' in disbelief, and raced through the rest of her interview with the reticule's original inhabitant, the foundling John Worthing, tearing up her notes by way of signalling the hopelessness of his quest.

Again, who would have supposed Dame Judi could make a success of Brecht's *Mother Courage*, as she did in Howard Davies's revival in 1984? Not even herself, because once again she accepted the director's invitation to play the part without knowing the play and was, she later said, extremely angry when she realised she'd be spending the evening pushing not just a cart but a very dodgy, cumbersome cart. But, boy, how she transformed herself for the role. A roughly chopped frizz of red hair topped a doughy face that, as often as not, was stuck in a combative pout from which flat, dour vowels emerged. Sometimes she scuttled over the stage like a scavenging cockroach, sometimes she ducked and weaved like a boxer, sometimes she simply stood, a frowzy, over-age punk waiting for something objectively awful but commercially gainful to happen.

Here, too, there was plenty of invention and, indeed, reinvention. In the famous scene when the battlefield survivor has to look at the body of her executed son, and pretend not to recognise him, Brecht's wife Helene Weigel ended up doing a great gaping imitation of the stricken horse in Picasso's *Guernica*. Dame Judi was less showy and, again, more truthful. She bent forward and further forward until her stony, numb-looking face became invisible, only a slight shudder of the body and an over-speedy shake of the head betraying what she really felt. And when her Mother Courage finally set off in search of the older son we know to be dead too, she moved us for what even Brecht, with his dogmatic insistence on 'alienation', would surely have agreed to be all the right reasons: she was still tough, still unsentimental, still unselfpitying, still unaware that her short-term opportunism had caused her family's everlasting destruction, still a remarkable example of human effort and human waste.

So, yes, Dame Judi can confound those who think of her primarily in warm, poignant, noble, or otherwise 'positive' roles: Hermione in *The Winter's Tale*, exuding as much dignified defiance as pain when she entered the court set up by her demented husband, or Deborah in Pinter's *A Kind of Alaska*, somehow overcoming her initial dismay and displaying a quiet, wise courage as she acknowledged that she'd been the twenty-nine-year victim of sleeping sickness, or O'Casey's Juno: exhausted, cynically aware of her 'paycock' husband's flaws and follies, yet brave, nurturing, resilient and innately so intelligent she made sense of the stage-direction which says that 'were circumstances favourable, she would probably be a handsome, active and clever woman'. As witness Dame Judi's Courage, her very common Dol Common in Jonson's *Alchemist*, her rowdy Christine in *Absolute Hell*, her debauched Mistress Quickly in Kenneth Branagh's film of *Henry V*, or her fierce, mocking Bessie Burgess in O'Casey's *Plough and the Stars*, she can be brash, blowsy or ugly when she needs to be.

But can she go still further into the darkness? It may seem

ungenerous to draw attention to what I regard as Dame Judi's one limitation in a book celebrating her achievements, but I suspect that she herself wouldn't wish that book to consist only of plaudits and praise, sweetness and light. The criticism she has sometimes attracted, that she's too 'nice' for this or that role, seems to me demonstrably wrong. But I've never seen her embody evil: meaning malignity and malice, pure selfishness or destructiveness for its own sake. If Mark Rylance asked her to play Iago in one of his women-only productions at Shakespeare's Globe – not an impossibility, because he admits to having tried and failed to persuade her to perform Brutus – I think she would do well to refuse.

In my view there's a good, principled reason for this limitation, if limitation it is. She finds it difficult to believe in an absolute or motiveless evil. She hated playing Regan, for instance, and did her best to explain what she admitted to thinking in-explicable, the sheer awfulness of Lear's most callous daughter. At the beginning of the performance she stammered and stuttered, infuriating the aggressive, impatient Lear, but found a new secur-ity and confidence with the coming of power over him. Her father's cruelty had, you felt, brought about her own cruelty. It's a perfectly legitimate interpretation, but it lacks Jacobean toughness and, in Dame Judi's case, it didn't quite add up. One moment she was a chillingly competent ward-sister, presiding over a radical eye-scrape, and the next she was reacting in horror to the killing of a husband she appeared to love and yet was required by Shakespeare promptly to forget in favour of the sexier Edmund.

She actually asked to be relieved of the role, as she did later with Gertrude in *Hamlet*, another character whose egregious behaviour she couldn't understand. She was also uneasy playing Portia, because she disliked the play, on the grounds that every-body in it, including herself, had to behave pretty badly. 'I'm not trying to whiten anyone,' she once said, apropos Regan. 'But it's boring to come on as an ugly sister and just be ugly. I'm interested in how someone becomes ugly. People aren't born wicked. It's what happens to them, the turn of the wheel. I need to know why they are the way they are.'

Does this mean that her professional instincts, which are to find some fellow-feeling and motivation for every character, as well as her own personal faith in the innate goodness of people, are sometimes in conflict with the facts as a pessimistic dramatist would see them? Perhaps. When I reviewed her Bianca in the RSC's revival of *Women Beware Women* in 1969 for the *New Statesman*, I was impressed by her nervous sexual surrender to Middleton's voracious Duke, her post-coital scruple, her growing self-confidence, her lingering affection for the husband she manages to doom. But I wrote: 'she never achieves the hardness of the poisoner she becomes.' Again, it's difficult to imagine her finding the icy vindictiveness to play Shakespeare's Queen Margaret, as the less versatile Peggy Ashcroft successfully did. And yet Dame Judi's need to explain, if not exactly to justify, is obviously a strength as well as a limitation.

Witness, above all, her Lady Macbeth.

It's not surprising that Dame Judi's performance of the character in 1976 was less in the tradition of Mrs Pritchard, the implacably grim, overpowering wife of Garrick's essentially decent Macbeth, than in that of Ellen Terry, whose Lady Macbeth selflessly gave support and strength to Henry Irving's sly, weak thane. Not that Ian McKellen, who played opposite her, was weak. Indeed, I'd rate his dark, stealthy, introverted Macbeth as the best I've seen. But he needed the right Lady, and he found her in Dame Judi, with the result that Trevor Nunn's production was also the most intimate and quietly powerful I can recall.

Dame Judi entered with a letter she'd clearly read a score of times, and began to steel herself to do business with 'murdering ministers' who both fascinated and terrified her, all for the sake of a man she loved. Again and again she fought her own fear and his doubts, encouraging him, soothing him, virtually mothering him when Duncan's murder looked like destroying his sense and sanity. But then – and there are barely noticeable lines which permit this – he began to rebuff and exclude her. And without the love that had motivated and sustained her, Dame Judi's Lady Macbeth gradually fell apart, ending up with a sleepwalking scene which left her weeping in agony as she relived the nightmare, trying actually to bite and suck the blood out of her hand, and, like some broken animal, emitting a long thin yowl of protest, a hoarse sigh that shook her whole body and, at one performance, so deprived her of oxygen that she passed out.

Better, surely, this subtle, scrupulously planned yet emotionally authentic reading than the out-front evil of the Mrs Pritchards. But this raises a new question. How does Dame Judi do it, not once, not twice, but night after night? Like most actresses, she resists talking about her craft, but, when I pushed her, she compared constructing a role to manning a giant console in which there are many more buttons to press than there are lines to deliver. Everything has to be considered during a rehearsal process that should be as open as possible: the intonation of each word, the essence of the character, the intentions of the author – 'and then you have to feel things, absolutely, in the gut, at the moment they occur'.

That implies an ability to react quickly and spontaneously to the shifting intonations or changing behaviour of other actors, and it's here that her fellow professionals especially value her and, in a modest way, she seems to value herself. She's done some fine things on the screen – who can forget her Mrs Brown or the baffled way in which her Iris Murdoch gradually disappeared into the mental void? – but it's the rapport of the theatre that means by far the most to her. She's quintessentially a company actor, so much so that the very idea of performing a solo or near-solo role, like Winnie in Beckett's *Happy Days*, apparently alarms and appals her.

And here's another set of contradictions. Judi Dench has sometimes been the company joker, often its leader and moral centre, and frequently both at once. As everyone in the profession knows, she is a prankster and, though she thinks she's less of a giggler than she once was, she still finds it hard to resist corpsing when something silly happens onstage. John Miller's biography of her contains many examples of this, and very funny they are. I suspect that largely they're evidence of that camaraderie: those who can laugh together will work better together. But her own testimony is that corpsing comes partly from that wry realism of hers, 'seeing how eccentric the whole business is', and partly from the nervous pressure she has always felt when she goes onstage.

Dame Judi isn't the only actor to admit to suffering from stage-fright. Olivier did so at times. Derek Jacobi and, even more seriously, Ian Holm have been disabled by it. But for Dame Judi the fear of letting down the audience, the author and herself is positively useful, because it produces the adrenalin that helps to explain her special combination of meticulousness and intensity. Stage-fright, she says, is necessary to her when she has to charge a character with terror, despair or another strong emotion. 'I would,' she says, 'be extremely frightened if I didn't feel fear.'

But, frightened or giggly or both, Dame Judi has as much moral authority as any actor or actress in the world. And I don't only or even mainly mean the obvious kind: giving encouragement, aid and, very occasionally, a word of reproach to her juniors. I mean something far subtler and, unlike the other sort, within the remit of a critic to discern. In fact, it's better described as a moral centredness or a spiritual integrity. It's not just a matter of trying sincerely to communicate profound human truths, though of course Dame Judi does that. It surely has as much to do with Judi Dench the person as with Judi Dench the actress, both of whom coexist in the unpindownable duality of the stage. Is it pretentious to say that behind her performances, and somehow irradiating them, is a steel of soul, a toughness of inner being? If so, I don't care, because I've felt it, there, in the flesh, in the theatre.

But let me end less enigmatically and more concretely, with a scattering of Dench moments I don't expect to forget. *Much Ado*:

Dame Judi's Beatrice, who had been troubling the audience with subtle signs of the unhappiness behind her surface merriment and embarrassing the court with the strength of the hostility she displayed towards Donald Sinden's Benedick, summoning him to dinner with a gong which she furiously banged while the confirmed bachelor, already duped into believing she loved him, maddened her by grinning in reply. Hugh Whitemore's *Pack of Lies*: Dame Judi gulping with a sort of intestinal horror as she launched into the process of betraying the close friend MI5 had told her was a Russian spy.

O'Casey's *Plough and the Stars*: Dame Judi's Bessie Burgess, lurching blotchy-eyed across the stage, her face squelched into a red scowl as she mocked her Catholic neighbours, yet suddenly, unexpectedly but believably finding the heart to help the one in the direst need. *The Duchess of Malfi*: Dame Judi's heroine exuding so much strength and light that, when she came to the famous words she had to utter in her extremity, 'I am Duchess of Malfi still,' she could afford to toss them out almost anti-climactically, as a simple fact of which others had to be softly and reasonably reminded.

So I might go on, finding example after example of Dame Judi's originality, wit, warmth or, to name the theatrical virtues she herself places at the top of the list, 'economy, simplicity'. But let's end by citing what, in 2004, was the most recent performance of all, her Countess of Rossillion in *All's Well That Ends Well*.

She was wise, emotionally munificent, tough, forgiving, grieving at times, yet always oddly serene. But what I think I'll especially remember is the episode when Dame Judi's Countess saw the much-loved daughter-figure and future daughter-in-law she had believed to be dead. And did she throb and gasp, boil and bubble? No, she thrust out her palms in a gesture of plain, unaffected joy. Believe me, only a very special actress could so effectively convince you at such a moment that less is more – and the understated can be overwhelming.

Early Days

BARBARA LEIGH-HUNT

Darling Jude,

Keith Waterhouse recently wrote that nostalgia isn't what it used to be – but frankly I take great pleasure in reminiscing about the time forty-seven years ago when I met someone who became and has remained a firm, close and much-loved friend.

It was in the late summer of 1957, the place was the Old Vic Theatre in the Waterloo Road in London where the resident company – under the artistic direction of Michael Benthall who was also directing the opening production of the season, *Hamlet* – was gathered together for rehearsals. The company was led by John Neville, Coral Browne and Jack Gwillim; I was a junior member of that august group, engaged for the season to walk on, understudy and play as cast.

Rehearsals had been under way for some days, but we were without an Ophelia when one morning, as the coffee break drew to a close, Michael Benthall led into our midst a diminutive young lady with long blonde hair dressed in a stylish chignon on her neck and announced, 'Ladies and gentlemen, may I introduce to you a young actress who is joining our company to play Ophelia – Judi Dench.'

You, poor girl, must have been terrified. You had recently graduated from the Central School of Speech and Drama with their Gold Medal, but here you were arriving at the stage door, which in those days was in the Waterloo Road, being met by the benign and kindness-personified stage-doorkeeper, Ernie Davis, who always had a warm greeting and wide smile for everyone, and knew everything that was happening in every department in the building, then being directed by him onto the side of the stage to await your introduction to the assembled cast.

Happily everyone received you with warm and friendly greetings, but we were all a little puzzled by the fact that this obviously attractive and dainty young woman had a face whose skin appeared to be navy-blue. Poor Judi, it transpired that your landlady at your bed-sitting room in Elm Park Gardens was washing your laundry with a soap powder to which you were allergic.

It was not long after joining us that you agreed to be the third tenant of a flat I was renting through friends Bryan Catley and Kenneth Thompson in Eaton Terrace, almost opposite the Antelope public house. It only had two bedrooms, so you and I had to share the large bedroom while Juliet Cooke, also in our company, occupied the smaller one. Juliet, like you, came from Yorkshire, she from Leeds, you from York; I represented the West Country, coming as I did from Bath. We all got on very well in our home under the eaves, reached by countless flights of stairs to attain our front door. It was modest in size, with a sitting room, bathroom and a very small kitchen that was really an overgrown cupboard, but we managed to produce some appetising meals in it. The flat itself was rather cold, no central heating in those days, but Juliet's family provided us with a fierce but effective oil heater, though of course we had to lug the oil for it up all those stairs.

We worked long hard hours, leaving the flat by 9.20 a.m. most days and not returning until well past 11.30 p.m., dog-tired and usually ravenously hungry. Then those stairs seemed neverending, and I recall you often saying wistfully in my ear, 'I wonder if anyone has delivered us a hamper from Fortnum & Mason?' Needless to say they never had, so we had then to turn to and conjure up something to assuage our hunger, doing our best not to awaken our landlord, Leslie Parker, in the process.

Michael Benthall and Robert Helpmann shared a garden flat

in Eaton Square just behind us, and some days Michael would kindly offer us a lift, thereby saving us the dash for the 46 bus from Sloane Square to the Waterloo Road. I remember one morning during one of those lifts Michael nearly crashed his car when we told him that we could see into their bedroom from our own bedroom. We failed to tell him that in order to do so we had to stand on the chest of drawers, and even then on a chair.

How happy those days were, and how we laughed until we ached. There were difficult times too – when Michael Langham came to rehearse us in *A Midsummer Night's Dream* and reduced us to tears almost daily – but we survived somehow, though I had almost forgotten it was supposed to be a comedy!

We enjoyed several visits from our families – your dear parents Reg and Olave coming from York, Juliet's parents from Leeds, and my mama from Bath – they all brought us more laughter, love and comfort, in practical ways too, armed with home-made goodies and warm clothing. You were unable to get home to York at weekends due to the railway timetable, no motorways then, so you took to coming home for the weekends with me to Bath, where my mama became for you the Other Mother, eventually just the OM.

Frequently a member of the company, Nicholas Meredith, would approach us on a Saturday, nervously twiddling a forelock of his hair, asking if we were catching the late train to the West Country and, if so, could we, would we, bring him back his usual request. This simply meant calling at a factory retail outlet near the station where the delectable chocolate Bath Oliver biscuits were made and sold; the famous cheese biscuits were thickly covered in a dark bitter chocolate and they were very more-ish, though you almost needed a hammer and chisel to break them. I recall that they also made a delicious sweet biscuit called Wheaten Malt, sadly discontinued when the factory was sold, which was a great shame, but we would return triumphantly with our purchase for the always grateful Nick.

So many names from those days come crowding back: Richard Gale, John Humphry, Jimmy Mellor, Miles Malleson, Moyra Fraser, Ronnie Fraser, Edward Hardwicke, Sarah Long, Neville Jason, Vernon Dobtcheff, Alec McCowen, David Dodimead, Derek Smith, Derek Francis, Jeffrey Wickham, Dennis Chinnery, George Little, Adrienne Hill, Paul Daneman, Jeremy Kemp, Jane Downs, Gerald Harper, Davina Beswick, Pinkie Johnstone, John Stride, Dyson Lovell, Peggy Mount, Job Stewart, Barbara Jefford, Margaret Courtenay, Gwen Watford, Fay Compton, Paul Rogers, Derek Godfrey, Norman Scase, Laurence Harvey, Donald Houston, Walter Hudd, John Moffatt, Frankie Howerd, Tommy Steele, Ann Bell, Joss Ackland, John Gielgud, Harry Andrews, Edith Evans, Harold Innocent, Jennie Goossens, Ursula Jenkins, Robert Young, Oliver Neville, David Gardner, Roy Patrick, Joseph O'Conor, Peter Hodgson, Peggy Butt, Dudley Jones, Sylvia Coleridge, Richard Wordsworth, Joyce Redman, Brian Spink, Rosalind Atkinson, Michael Culver, Michael Meacham, Peter Cellier, and two dressers who went on to become well-established actors – Sebastian Breaks and Stephen Moore.

I remember Maggie Smith rushing to catch her train connection for the Isle of Wight every Saturday, and Coral Browne insisting upon taking you into the house where she and her husband Philip Pearman lived in Chester Terrace when you succumbed to flu, as she was afraid that our flat was too cold and there was no one there during the day to nurse you, which she then proceeded to do herself.

There was Stanley Meadows who was a little physically clumsy through sheer eagerness, and whenever there was a crash or clatter back-stage Coral would say, 'Oh Gawd, there goes Stanley Meadows again!'; Charles West who was able somehow to go to sleep standing up when playing one of the countless Bishops in *Henry VIII*, resting his head piously on his crozier; Barrie Ingham making us giggle onstage by suddenly waggling his moustache held by wires in his mouth; and our dear dresser Maudie, who in her heyday had been a Bluebell Girl but now, although tall, had thickened a little, and her once beautiful legs troubled her a lot, all that dancing I suppose. During *Hamlet*, towards the end of the evening she'd knock on our dressing room door and ask, 'Miss 'Unt, has Fortingrass gone on yet?' That was her licence to put on her hat and coat, ready to make her exit speedily.

I recall you buying Douglas – later Paul – Harris's MG sports car, and driving with you down the King's Road and you saying, 'Oh, look, there's a lovely dress in that window, and there's a smashing suit over there, and what a pretty pair of shoes.' I was a nervous wreck!

I also remember us driving Pinkie Johnstone to London Airport, as she was flying to New York to appear in *Five Finger Exercise*. It was an awful day, black clouds and quite a wind. We had Davina Beswick, a company colleague with us, and on the way back somewhere in what Margaret Rutherford's beloved husband Stringer Davis called 'Roundaboutia' we broke down on a dual carriageway lined with wide grass verges and semi-detached houses. Having found a phone-box to request help from the AA, which they promised to provide, we sat there shivering as Davina inveighed against 'the bloody smug houses with their dimity curtains'. I think you and I would have been quite happy to have sheltered in one of them at the time. Then to our horror a police car stopped, and two young PCs got out to ask if we needed assistance. We assured them it was on the way, and off they went, only to come back several times to see if we were all right. How we dreaded them saying, 'Perhaps we'd better just see your licence.' Years later I passed my driving test – I was a late developer – and phoned you to tell you. You were incensed that I'd done it before you: 'You haven't, Bar? You haven't!!' Shortly after that you passed yours, so that was all right.

Then of course there's our old friend Delia – not Smith, the one from *The Merry Widow* – she was responsible for the only real disagreement we had, and it really was rather trivial. You came home one day, this time it was in your flat in Regent's Park, to find me drying up some dishes and warbling this song. You asked what it was and when I replied 'Vilya' you insisted that it was 'Delia', and after a lengthy argument you rang Pinkie, who agreed with me. To this day 'Vilya' haunts us. The phone will ring and we invite each other to tune the radio to the required channel; when the correct contact is made, down goes the receiver.

Going back to the close of our first season at the Old Vic, the company was travelling the next day to Paris as part of a tour that was to take us also to Antwerp and Brussels. We couldn't afford to keep on the flat while we were abroad, so we drove away from the theatre in a taxi to go home to pack and clean the flat. At about 2 a.m. we were on our hands and knees cleaning our bedroom floor when I began to laugh helplessly; I think it was fatigue and the sight of you, bless you, polishing away, while all those fans were obviously convinced that you were wining and dining at some glamorous restaurant.

When we returned from our tour another friend in the company, Crispian Woodgate, helped us to find some short-term accommodation, a huge, cheerless and rather bleak bed-sitting room in Notting Hill. I believe we then went off on tour to the USA and Canada, after which I went into rep, and you found your flat in Regent's Park. It was there, I remember, that we heard of the death of President Kennedy on the radio just as I was leaving for the theatre. I was playing in *A Severed Head* at the Criterion Theatre at the time, and that night at the end of the performance we played the American National Anthem, and the news was still so fresh that many people didn't understand why it had been played.

We've managed to appear together down the years. Do you recall that when we were in *Pack of Lies* at the Lyric Theatre with darling Mike, the phone rang one evening after the curtain-call and the stage-doorkeeper said, 'There's a Mr Howerd for you both'? He knocked on the dressing room door, and there was Frankie saying rather nervously, 'Do you remember me?'

Then I 'married' you and Geoffrey Palmer in *As Time Goes By*, recalling my own marriage to Richard in Bath Register Office, when you and Richard's Uncle Horace were our 'bridesmaids', and you gloriously punctuated the ceremony by the buttons popping off your coat several times, and we all, including the Registrar, fell to our knees to retrieve them.

Happy and joyous occasions – your wedding to Mike in that glorious church just round the corner from your dear house in Hampstead, and walking to and from the ceremony; the birth of Finty, and learning to be brave enough to bath and hold that tiny scrap of girlhood who used to love to cling onto a silver bracelet I used to wear; and now the next generation manifesting itself in Sam, who is so like Mike, but with red hair, that it is uncanny.

There have been so many happy times, but oh how I wish, dear one, that you could have been spared the sad ones. But the bravery and sheer guts with which you have faced the tragedies and adversities which have assailed you, and the joy you get from life, and share so readily and generously with others is a lesson to us all. I feel blessed to have shared so much with you, and hope that as you continue to scale the heights you have ever more joy and happiness ahead.

In admiration, of which I hope you are in no doubt whatever,
And ever lovingly,
Bardle

Arousing Admiration

IAN RICHARDSON

When I first met Judi Dench in 1962, she was already an old Shakespeare hand. During her time at the Old Vic she had played Juliet, Isabella, Viola – to name but a few, whereas I, apart from a juvenile Hamlet at the Birmingham Repertory Theatre, was struggling along with lords and underlings. By 1962 I had been slightly promoted and was rehearsing Oberon, with Judi as Titania. Peter Hall told me my verse was leaden. That I didn't fly. Judi was all air and fire, and I was all earth. It was rather like those long-vanished schooldays, when the master would cry despairingly: 'I don't know why you can't spell anything right/add two and two/remember who won the Wars of the Roses . . . Why can't you be like so-and-so? So-and-so *always* gets it right. Perhaps so-and-so could help you.' And you looked at so-and-so, and you just *hated* them. Well, it was a bit like that with me and Judi, except, of course that no one could possibly hate her. So, I humbled myself and listened and learned. Oh, and I took my shoes off, which helped.

That season, as well as Titania, she was a luminous Isabella in *Measure for Measure.* Anyone who has ever worked with Judi knows that she is one of the world's greatest gigglers. No matter what the play, just beneath the surface and waiting to burst is a bubble of laughter which, strangely enough, does not at all detract from her playing of tragedy: if anything, it enhances it. I was playing Lucio, a bit of no-good lowlife, who has to come on and break the bad news that Isabella's brother has been sentenced to death for fornication. The line is: 'Your brother and his lover have embraced ...' One evening, in a moment of aberration, I came out with 'Your lover and his brother have embraced ...' A ramification of the plot which would have totally altered the behaviour of the protagonists. Judi disappeared so far upstage that she was almost out of sight, leaving me frantically trying to work out if I should correct myself or plough on regardless, while she heaved silently, head averted, and didn't help at all.

And she was no better offstage in private life. In the Stratford of that day the High Street was still full of old-fashioned shops: no Debenhams, no Accessorize, no fast fooderies. The sole survivors, the Garrick Inn, which used to have a great copper stove in the middle of the snug, for the comfort of cold actors, and the Hathaway Tea Rooms with its window full of scones, now jostle with the newer retailers with an air of unease. The Elizabethan house, where generations of young actors stayed in digs with the miraculous singing teacher, Denne Gilkes (who had known Yeats), is now a restaurant and the chemist near the corner of Bridge Street, whose name can still be seen above the mobile phones in the window, has long gone. And here is the point of my preamble. This chemist was called Loggins and thither Judi went one day to buy cotton wool for taking off her make-up. She couldn't see any in the body of the shop and the assistant said that she didn't think they had any, but were 'waiting for a delivery'. At this point, like a jack-in-the-box, Mr Danks the pharmacist bobbed his head round the corner of the dispensary. 'Oh, Miss Dench!' he called, as Judi started to leave, 'I've got coloured balls!' The passing tourists and townspeople must have wondered why this distinguished actress appeared to be having hysterics in the High Street. And she was still laughing when she arrived at the theatre some quarter of a mile later.

So keeping a straight face in Judi's company is a difficult business. But it doesn't matter. You know that old saying about not acting with children and animals? Well, you can add 'or Judi Dench'. Because nobody's going to look at you while she's on.

Years later, when she was rehearsing *The Winter's Tale*, playing both Hermione and Perdita, I met her back-stage. I wasn't in the production, but my seven-year-old son, Jeremy, was playing Mamillius and I had come to fetch him when I bumped into Judi in the back dock. She was in tears. 'What's the matter?' 'Oh, Trevor won't let me laugh . . . and I *have* to laugh in rehearsal or nothing will work.' Well, perhaps he did let her laugh because the performance certainly worked. I can remember to this day her slow-motion faint as Hermione when Leontes refuses to believe the Oracle's message that she is innocent of adultery. There were strobe lights and everything became dreamlike and unreal, the white figure collapsing in a death-like faint. The sheer physical and technical skill of that, *to fall in slow motion*, arouses the admiration, never mind the acting. As Perdita, which she played with a Yorkshire accent – a nod towards her roots – she was a joyous and golden girl and quite believably a shepherdess.

She was very kind to my son Jeremy, especially after the showing of the televised version. By this time, the play had moved to the Aldwych. We all sat and watched the transmission (it must have been a Sunday) and Jeremy saw himself for the first time. And thought he was dreadful. Come the next performance, his head was down, his voice had disappeared and Judi and all her ladies-in-waiting had to jolly him along, sit him on their knees and tell him he was wonderful. Strangely, my second son, Miles, has recently been acting with Judi in *All's Well That Ends Well*. She was very kind to him, too, but I don't suppose she let him sit on her knee. He's over forty.

Some time after the stage presentation, we filmed *A Midsummer Night's Dream*. The location chosen for the entire shoot was Compton Verney, east of Stratford-upon-Avon and convenient for the theatre where most of us were currently appearing. The lovely old house had been derelict for years, occupied for a time by the army, and then left to rot. But the 120 acres of wood and parkland were a superbly versatile setting for all the cinematic requirements. (Incidentally, at the time of writing, I have just read that the estate has been purchased by a millionaire business-man and transformed into an art gallery.) The time of year was autumn and the dank little wood in which we were filming was chill and cheerless, in spite of the designer having come in, tut-tutted about the colour of the trees, and sprayed them all another colour. The costumes had been totally altered. Whereas before we fairies had been silvery echoes of the Jacobean mortals, we were now almost stark naked. I wore boots and a wig. Judi wore a small amount of ivy with the odd strand or two of chamois leather and we were both covered in a thin layer of bright green make-up. It was incredibly cold. It had been arranged that, for the speech that is usually identified as 'the nine-men's morris', where Titania bemoans the fact that the weather is dreadful because she and Oberon have quarrelled, we should stand on the shores of the ornamental lake.

It was almost the only day since we'd started when it wasn't raining, and Peter Hall wanted rain. The Warwickshire Fire Brigade had therefore been engaged to play their hoses onto the lake behind us. Because of our nakedness, and the intense cold, we were huddled in blankets, which we only discarded just before the cry of 'Action!' Judi's blanket being hurled to one side revealed her to the hitherto uninitiated fireman to all intents and purposes starkers. The young man holding the hose goggled. His jaw dropped. So, unfortunately, did the hose, catching us both amid-ships and washing us into the lake, from whose muddy verges we were eventually plucked, helpless with laughter and extremely filthy. The Fire Chief was furious – 'Why don't you keep your eyes on the job?' he bellowed. Filming had to be abandoned for the day.

Apart from the odd charity performance or poetry reading, these were the only times that I worked with Judi and, in a way, I knew Michael better. When the newly christened Royal Shakespeare Company branched out from its Stratford base and moved into the Aldwych, we all had to find places to live. I had the good fortune to find a huge mansion flat in Prince of Wales

Drive, where there was plenty of room in spite of my having by this time acquired a wife and two children. Michael had joined the company in 1963 and had taken over from Ian Holm as Puck, Titania by this time being played by Juliet Mills. He had nowhere to live. 'Do you think I could come and stay for a week, while I find a flat?' 'Of course . . .' Six months later, when we left London for a long foreign tour, he still hadn't found anywhere. He was a lovely lodger, even though his culinary tastes at that time were a little conservative.

'What's for dinner?' he'd ask. My wife Maroussia, who is an excellent cook, would say blanquette de veau or bœuf bourguignon or whatever it was, and Michael would pause slightly and say, 'Do you think I could just have an egg butty?'

He was very attractive, with an insouciant and largely unconscious sex appeal, and there was no shortage of girls living in hope. And not only girls. Just round the corner from the Aldwych was Covent Garden, and one admirer used to come and wait for him at the stage door. Michael was flattered, given the stratospheric fame of Rudolf Nureyev, but at the same time felt rather uncomfortable. How could he imply, without insulting the great man, that his interests didn't lie quite in the same direction?

I suppose that by that time, he and Judi had met, as the members of the company always seemed to know each other, even if some were at the Aldwych and some at Stratford, but they had not yet come together. Loving them both separately, it was a truly joyous day when we heard they were to marry. I was an usher at their wedding, along with Alec McCowen. We had played twins in *The Comedy of Errors* and amazingly turned up at the church in almost identical grey suits and wearing pink roses in our buttonholes. Michael, resplendent in a suit and a Beatles haircut, was hovering nervously. 'When you see her coming,' he said, 'could you give a wave to cue the music?' So I kept watch. From afar approached the largest bouquet you have ever seen, almost obscuring the person carrying it. I got ready to wave but . . . no! It turned out to be Danny La Rue. Judi, who arrived shortly afterwards, looking straight out of a fairytale, actually carried a very *small* posy. After the service we all went to a reception at the zoo, which was an obvious and appropriate choice of venue, for Judi adores animals.

Visiting her recently, at her lovely Surrey home, I had come in by the gate that I'd been told to, found the parking area, but couldn't actually see the house. Enter a friendly cat, who greeted me and led the way along a leafy and partly obscured path to the front door, looking over his shoulder from time to time to make sure I was following. 'He's the new car-park attendant,' said Judi. 'The previous one resigned for some reason.'

I had gone to her house to rehearse a poetry reading which we were to give as part of the Stratford Poetry Festival. It was nearly forty years since we had been together in the theatre in Stratford and it was a very strange feeling to walk into our old dressing rooms on the first floor – well, not quite walk in, since they now have security codes that you have to punch in and we kept on forgetting our numbers – to look out of the window at the swans who have been joined in the interim by hundreds of Canada geese, and to note the subtle changes. 'There's a fridge!' 'I wonder if you can still talk to each other down the plughole in the bath?' 'The loo seems to have got smaller.' After a little, Judi bounced in to consult on her wardrobe. 'What do you think?' The choice was between a long black skirt with a matching top and stole, or the identical thing with trousers and she modelled them both for me. We decided that the trouser suit was best. 'It could probably go on and do the recital by itself,' said Judi. 'It's done enough of them.' We visited each other, calming our nerves, for the time remaining until curtain up. 'Now, you won't sit on your own during the interval, will you?' No, of course not.

Writing about Judi is always going to be to wallow in super-latives. The wretched woman has no faults, either personally or professionally. Mrs Wonderful, that's her. Over the years, I have marvelled at the subtlety and, in some ways, the simplicity of her acting. What she does seems to be the right and only thing to do at the moment she does it. And it doesn't look at all like acting. In the above-mentioned poetry reading, of which the subject was 'childhood', there was one piece where she, as a very small girl, was sitting at a dining table, a bit too high for her, waiting and hoping that she would get a piece of cake. As yet again she was given a piece of bread, and the plate with the cakes was exhausted before it reached her, and she tried not to cry; as she watched the birthday cake being cut and longing to get one of the bits with the icing on ... but you knew she wouldn't ... It was perfection.

Utterly Aware

RICHARD EYRE

I'm looking at a photograph of four adults and two children – young boys – lined up on one side of a large kitchen table. They are watching six clockwork chicks (it's Easter) racing across the table. Bets have been laid; the form of the chicks is unpredictable. One charges forward then falls on its beak, one stutters in circles, one mounts the rear of another, one never moves. The faces of the players are infused with sporting passion, but one face is contorted, no, not contorted, illuminated by demented glee. It's Judi Dench, in an ecstasy of fun, combining three of her favourite things: love of company, love of games and love of betting. It's not perhaps the image that most people have of someone who, as the Japanese say, is a Living National Treasure, but it's closer than the weird caricature of gentility that is sometimes touted in the press – what Billy Connolly describes as 'those English twittering fucking women – they think she's one of them, and she isn't.'

Alan Bennett is also a Living National Treasure. We were once speculating about what was the world's worst-taste T-shirt. Alan said he'd recently seen a young man wearing a Heavy Metal T-shirt that read HITLER: THE EUROPEAN TOUR. 'That's bad,' I said. 'That's awful, but what about one that I saw shortly after thirty-nine Turin football fans had been killed in an accident at a soccer match against Liverpool that read: LIVERPOOL 39 TURIN 0.' 'Yes, that's ghastly,' said Alan. 'But the worst-taste T-shirt, the very worst,' he said, 'would be one that read: I HATE JUDI DENCH.' Most of us have been wearing our 'I LOVE JUDI DENCH' T-shirts for years. Mine's a bit grey by now; I've been wearing it since 1966.

That was the year I first saw Judi act. It wasn't onstage, it was on TV, a four-part drama by John Hopkins called *Talking to a Stranger*, directed by Christopher Morahan. I still think it's one of the few authentic television masterpieces. It was about a suburban family disintegrating over a weekend, seen through the eyes of each of its members: father, mother, daughter, son. The performances of the actors – Maurice Denham, Margery Mason, Michael Bryant – are vivid still in my mind but the image of Judi is something more than vivid: it has an aura, a corona like the glow around a high-voltage element. In a room in Dorset, watching on a small black-and-white TV set, I was dazzled by her passionate energy, her abandon, her vulnerability and her sharp wit. She was a star.

It says everything about Judi and as much about the era that she didn't immediately gravitate to films. But this was the age of 'dolly birds' and 'swinging London' and all the tatty crap that makes it difficult to be nostalgic about the sixties, unless you were stoned all the time, living in Ibiza, or both, and film producers (with Samantha Eggar as their role model) recoiled from this mercurial, round-faced young actor who could move from laughter to tears in the blink of an eye.

And the theatre presented her with a world in which she was, if not entirely in control of her destiny in the choice of parts, wholly in control of it when she was acting. The theatre is a world where you can learn from night to night, where you don't have to conform to a physical type, where you have the power to convince an audience that you are whoever you choose to be. The theatre thrives on metaphor – a room becomes a world, a group of characters becomes a whole society – and in enlisting the imagination of the audience an actor performs an act of poetry. A passion for poetry – intensity of beauty in language and gesture – is in Judi's genes.

Later that year I saw her on the stage for the first time. It was in a production of *Richard II*; John Neville was playing the King. Judi was not actually supposed to be in the show, but had appeared – it was a midweek matinee – as a conspicuously small soldier guarding the imprisoned monarch. She was dressed from top to toe in chain-mail with a helmet on her head that looked like a metal mixing-bowl. One by one the actors realised that they were sharing the stage with her and a contagious frenzy gripped the whole company. They shuddered in unison, legless with laughter. Only John Neville, to Judi's fury, defiantly resisted the bait and, in spite of the distraction, I still remember his performance as one of the best I've ever seen in a Shakespeare play.

This happened at Nottingham Playhouse where Judi was playing Amanda in *Private Lives*, which alternated in the repertoire with the Shakespeare. I was working at the theatre, directing a schools' tour of Goldoni's *Mirandolina*. It was my first job as a director and I owed it, in part, to Judi. I had been working in the nearby city of Leicester the previous Christmas at the Phoenix Theatre. I was a disaffected member of the chorus in an uncomfortable production of a musical for which I had no great affection, *The Boy Friend.* In order to deflect my growing despair (and that of some of my fellow cast) I directed a production of *The Knack*, by Ann Jellicoe, to be played for one Sunday night. By some special providence John Neville came to see the production with Judi, liked what he saw and offered me the job in Nottingham.

Which is how I came to meet Judi and began a friendship which will last until I fail to come round to her dressing room and be generous after a show – something I did once and for which she's never forgiven me. My crime – and it was a crime – was a failure of good manners which for Judi is much more than obeying common courtesies, writing thank you letters, sending cards of condolence and remembering birthdays, though all those as well. Her notion of good behaviour – of 'acting well', if you

One of the youngest members of the Old Vic Company, 1957.

Anya in *The Cherry Orchard*, with John Gielgud as Gaev.
Royal Shakespeare Company, 1961.

*'Already at that age lit up from inside, speaking to each of us
individually and all of us collectively – both at the same time.'*

Titania in *A Midsummer Night's Dream*, with Ian Richardson
as Oberon. Royal Shakespeare Company, 1962.

'Judi was all air and fire.'

Isabella in *Measure for Measure*. Royal Shakespeare Company, 1962.

'She was a luminous Isabella.'

Viola in *Twelfth Night*. Royal Shakespeare Company, 1969.

'She's without parallel when it comes to suggesting love's intricacies and contradictions.'

Backstage during *London Assurance*. Royal Shakespeare Company, 1972. The part she finally had to relinquish to give birth to Finty.

$\mathcal{W}$ith Finty twenty-nine years later – when she was awarded
the BAFTA Fellowship on her birthday, 9 December 2001.

Adriana in *The Comedy of Errors*, with Michael Williams as one of the Dromio twins. Royal Shakespeare Company, 1976.

'Full of immensely skilled and endearing performances.'

like – is tied up with what makes her such a good actor: her ability to empathise with other people, to imagine what a person, real or fictional, is feeling. It's what the French philosopher Simone Weil called the gift of compassion: 'The love of our neighbour means being able to say: What are you going through? It is a recognition that the sufferer exists as a person exactly as you are. The laws of necessity are as unexceptional as the laws of gravity. The human faculty of compassion opposes this order and is therefore best thought of as being in some way supernatural. To forget oneself briefly, to identify with a stranger to the point of fully recognising him or her, is to defy necessity.'

Judi's philosophy is a sort of Christian one but it's less a set of beliefs – she's a practising Quaker – than an instinct to defy necessity by loving her neighbour in the way Simone Weil describes. Judi acts well in life and in her work, but while acting well on stage is difficult and demanding, it's an admirable but far from unique gift. What is rare – very rare – is for an actor to square the circle of work and life.

What are the things I remember most clearly of Judi when I first met her? Alone among my friends she always called me Rich (and still does) and I asked her to be in a play that I had written which she turned down without breaking my heart, even when hers was so busy being broken. She was always in love or falling in love, and sometimes both at the same time and usually with the wrong man, unsuitable but irresistible. She was like Ranevskaya in *The Cherry Orchard*: 'What do I do? I fall in love with his double.' When we did the play for BBC TV years later she said to me, 'I've cast this man in Paris, this man who's made her so unhappy, you know who, don't you, Rich?' I did.

She was always a romantic and she still is, by which I mean she believes in the redeeming power of love. Being a romantic doesn't mean she's sentimental, even if there's a side of her that to a mean-spirited observer – the sort who calls actors 'luvvies' – might seem soppy: the first night cards, soft toys, soft hearts and easy endearments that make up the stew of back-stage life which, for all its superficiality, is threaded with genuine affection and appreciation of the value of real comradeship.

And with Judi, laughter, a sound somewhere between a chuckle and a gurgle – sexy and subversive – is always bubbling up. She has an impish sense of humour. When we were rehearsing *The Cherry Orchard* she sent me a Christmas card in the shape of a man in a gorilla suit. And on the last night of *A Little Night Music* she faced Larry Guittard (whom we'd brought over from New York for the show), opened her dressing gown and revealed the words 'Go home, Yank' written on a bodystocking. And she thinks nothing of conscripting several dozen people to send mocking postcards to an actor friend to whom she'd given a twenty-pound note to pay for a short taxi ride and overheard say: 'You can keep the change.' 'Thank *you*, guv,' said the justly astonished taxi driver.

She revels in banter, bonhomie and practical jokes, yet behind that wholly accessible, almost excessively generous façade there's an intensely private, even unreachable, person; what Franco Zeffirelli called 'a secret garden'. It's one of the many paradoxes of her character: she's hard-headed but big-hearted, subversive but respectful of tradition, insecure but defiant in the face of fear, wildly passionate but almost always temperate. I've only once seen her very angry. A journalist in the *Daily Telegraph* had suggested that she was scene-stealing, systematically upstaging the other actors by ostentatiously moving props. You'd need to be very stupid and have a wilful ignorance of Judi's character to believe that she would behave so ungenerously to her fellow actors. She was volcanically angry, so angry that she became white-faced and the tips of her ears glowed red. If she had confronted the journalist at that moment, murder would have been too good for her.

Paradoxes are the oxygen of good actors: you have to seek attention for yourself but you can't be narcissistic, you have to perform but not show off, you have to communicate but in someone else's voice, and if you don't find the balance between these opposites, acting is just showing off. But to play one thought while thinking three or four others and moving dexterously around a stage or film set is the essential professional requirement. No less essential requirements for life as an actor are resilience and fortitude. They breed stoicism: grace under pressure, as Hemingway called it. 'An actor must affect an immoderate buoyancy of spirits while perhaps his heart is breaking,' said the actor Macready, and no one could have followed his dictum more earnestly than Judi when we filmed *Iris* not many weeks after Michael's death. Mike had been her north, south, east and west, more so than I had realised, and her grief was a terrible thing to witness. Grief can make you cruel; with Judi it made her determined, producing a ferocious energy that translated into an unusual immersion in preparing for the part. This involved a previously untried approach: reading the script before she started to work on it.

In the past she has recklessly courted disaster by insisting on starting with a blank page so that the whole of the process – from the acceptance of the part until the end of the read-through on the first day of the rehearsals – has been a blindfold journey, where she's innocent of what's around each corner. She wouldn't even use Denholm Elliott's test for accepting a role: 'I open a script in the middle,' he said to me once, 'and if I think there's anybody in it that I'd like to have a drink with, I turn back to the beginning and read it.' Not Judi: she'd ask someone to paraphrase the script for her or just rely on her sense of smell – and I'm not sure I'm being metaphorical.

With *Iris*, because the period leading up to it was a period of forced unemployment while she was caring for Michael, she departed from her normal preparation for a part, which is to rely almost entirely on her instincts and, through a process of osmosis, soak up the details and absorb the character's life without allowing anything of herself to encroach on the character. To prepare for playing Iris Murdoch she read the script (two drafts even) and watched a documentary. She was fascinated by Iris Murdoch's accent, particularly the way she sounded the 'h' in words like 'which' or 'whist', as she does herself. Discovering that their mothers were from the same background, genteel Dublin Protestants, was another point of access to the character.

More typical of her approach to studying a part was to sit in the car when we were filming in Oxford outside the house that John Bayley had shared with Iris Murdoch. What she gleaned from this was their indifference to possessions: the windows of the house were open and his dusty little car was in the driveway, unlocked, while he was away. She accumulates small details like a detective, asks you questions that seem barely relevant to the character she's playing, then leaves you as soon as you answer, as if she'd disturbed you while you were reading a book, afraid that talking about it more will muddy her instinct. It was through intuition rather than study that she achieved that alchemical physical transformation at the end of *Iris*, when her eyes became vacant but her soul still seemed at home. She didn't go to old people's homes to observe patients suffering from Alzheimer's disease; she asked little about my mother, who had had a cruelly long decay into the terminal stage, and she talked for a short time to an old friend of hers who was in the very early stages of the illness. The rest – the progressive descent into oblivion – she guessed.

Judi works through doubt, scepticism and guesswork and, like a prospector panning for gold in a stream, is never content until she's found something solid. The way she works is entirely idiosyncratic. It's like Churchill's description of Russia: a riddle wrapped in a mystery inside an enigma. Like all good actors she doesn't really have a method, still less *The* Method. One of the things I dislike about *The* Method is that with its catechism of 'impro', 'emotional memory', 'private moments' and 'relaxation exercises' it's become a credo rather than a process. Actors become more concerned with finding themselves than the author's character. All acting 'methods' have to be empirical, they're just means to an end; if they're codified, like Stanislavsky's and Lee Strasberg's, the means become the end.

Some actors lose themselves in research as if to elevate the business of acting into a pseudo-science, others improvise and paraphrase, others literally become the character, on set and off. Others get drunk. The aim, whether it's in theatre, film or television, Shakespeare, Scorsese or *EastEnders*, is to be – or more importantly to *appear* to be – spontaneous: you have to look as though the thoughts and words and feelings and actions are occurring for the first time. However it's achieved, all actors have to keep a corner of their brain actively deployed as a monitor, cold, detached, critical and unengaged. It's their third eye, that facility for being utterly aware of what they're doing and yet appearing utterly unselfconscious and innocently spontaneous. That's what the job is, Judi would say. Nobody does it better.

She has technique to burn – she can turn a line on a fragment of a syllable, a scene on the twist of a finger – but her technique never shows. She has the ear of a musician and the eye of a painter. With her voice, that bluesy alto, she can bend a note from joy to a sob and she has a dancer's dexterity, always using her body expressively. In film they say you should hold everything in, in theatre the opposite. But Judi breaks the rules, in any medium she seems mercurial and yet constant, she's entirely open yet never lets you feel – as in life – that you've glimpsed the whole person. David Hare wrote a speech for a character in *Amy's View* that describes this phenomenon. With astonishing prescience it was written before Judi had been cast: 'it may be presumptuous but I feel I'm beginning to understand your technique ... You never play anything outwards. I've noticed you keep it all in. So you draw in the audience. So it's up to them. And somehow they make the effort ... They have to go and get it themselves. What I don't know is, how do you do it?'

The answer is: I really don't know. In rehearsal the elements of her performance seem disparate but gradually and invisibly the elements come together: head, heart, voice and body into a marvellous harmony, never a wasted gesture, never a superfluous move. She always reminds me of what a famous English play-agent called Peggy Ramsay told me once about recognising whether an actor is in character: 'Look at the feet, dear.'

When I was editing *Iris* the editor was reluctant to cut the clapper board off the beginning of one take. At the beginning of the shot (a close-up of Judi) you could see Judi laughing – she'd been telling a joke – then you could hear my voice – '... and ... action' – and within four frames, that's one-sixth of a second, there was a woman in the latter stages of decay from Alzheimer's disease, or more to the point there *wasn't* a woman, there was an absence of a woman, totally vanished behind the eyes. It was like watching a musician rehearse. 'Bar 34,' says the conductor, gives the downbeat and the soloist and orchestra pick up on the first note of the bar, no shuffling, no prevarication: pitch and tempo perfect.

I think Judi is a genius and I know exactly how she would react if I said so to her face. 'Oh, Rich,' she'd say and shrug like a cat arching its back. And then she'd laugh. That word 'genius' is rather debased currency. We tend to sprinkle it about like Italian waiters with peppermills. But I think it's accurate to call Judi a genius, because she's one of those people, like Oscar Peterson or Yehudi Menuhin or Cary Grant, who appear to do what they do brilliantly as if it cost them nothing, as if it was effortless. Judi acts like Matisse draws, never taking his hand from the page.

Once, at the end of a day's rehearsal after the actors had left the room, the stage manager held up a script and called out to me in horror: 'Judi's left her script.' At the time I think I was shocked too that Judi could be so cavalier, but now I understand that it's her way: she harvests the part in rehearsals, lets it ferment outside. Only when we were doing *Amy's View,* for the first time in her life she found that her way was failing her. Tired from promoting a film and from every other call on her seemingly inexhaustible well of energy, she wasn't picking up the lines in rehearsals. She found she had to take her script home and learn her lines in the bath. She was sufficiently worried to tell me that she thought she'd have to withdraw from the play. She wasn't using her pessimism as a charm to ward off ill spirits; the insecurity was genuine and she overcame it. It was only then that I realised that a controlled sense of panic underlies all her work: the way she chooses her parts, the way she rehearses, the way she performs.

Why does she act? Maybe there's no more sufficient answer than the existential proposition: because that's what she does because she was born to do it. All actors act because they want their existence to be corroborated: they want to be seen, they want approval, but however fine the actor's performance and however distant the characterisation from the actor's personality, the audience doesn't draw a fine line between approving the performance and approving the actor. So in seeking approval the actor is seeking love. If this implies a childhood devoid of affection, it's hard to square with Judi, who was loved and encouraged by her parents and has a way of capsizing everyone she meets with affection.

All of us ask ourselves: am I loved? Judi's acting is an attempt to answer this question of others and of herself. Every part she takes on has to test her; it has to be something that she thinks she might not be able to do. Every time she acts she has to feel just enough fear to keep self-love at bay and needs to find affirmation from the audience. The lure of acting – of doing something really well – is that when she's finished a performance there's a sense of triumph over the fear: danger is overcome and love is requited. She'd be frightened if she wasn't frightened. While there's danger and insecurity there can never be boredom, which could be why she's still at the peak she's been at since she played Juliet in 1957.

Iris was a film about enduring love. It wouldn't and couldn't have been made without Judi as an actor and as a person. It was her character, as much as that of Iris Murdoch (or at least the Iris Murdoch mediated through John Bayley's accounts of her), that was at the heart of the film. When I was writing the screenplay with Charles Wood, we decided to end the film with Iris redux, a lecture given in her prime cross-cut with her dying on a hospital bed, both watched lovingly by her husband. Her lecture was a paraphrase of a lecture Iris Murdoch had given, but it could just as easily have been improvised by Judi:

Human beings love each other, in sex, in friendship, and when they are in love, and they cherish other beings – humans, animals, plants, even stones. The quest for happiness and the promotion of happiness is in all of this, and the power of our imagination. We need to believe in something divine without the need for God, something which we might call Love or Goodness. Indeed as the psalm says: 'Whither shall I go from thy spirit, whither shall I flee from thy presence? If I ascend unto heaven thou art there, if I make my bed in hell behold thou art there. If I take the wings of the morning and dwell in the uttermost parts of the sea, even there shall thy hand lead me, and thy right hand shall hold me.'

Body Language

STANLEY WELLS

On February 2004, while Judi was appearing in Stratford as the Countess of Rossillion in *All's Well That Ends Well*, I took part in a public conversation with her at the Shakespeare Centre. This is the headquarters of the Shakespeare Birthplace Trust, of which Judi is a Life Trustee. We are only one of literally hundreds of charitable organisations to which she gives her generous support, and we have often been able to call on her for practical help. Over the Christmas period and later she had been appearing at numerous public functions in the area, opening the public library, reading at carol services, and the like – as well as giving seven performances a week and entertaining the many friends and admirers who came from far and wide to see the play – so it was with some hesitation that I asked her to undertake yet another engagement. But she agreed with her usual grace, and within two or three days of the announcement of the event, every seat in our largest hall was sold. We laid on a relay with a video link in an adjoining room, and before long that too had sold out. Before the event began she gave an interview and a photo call to the local newspaper. I led her into the main hall through the smaller one, and of course she was rapturously greeted in both.

In our public conversation Judi expressed her fondness for Stratford and its neighbourhood, and later, as we lunched together, she told me that during the previous weeks she had taken solitary drives into the local countryside, reminding herself of the Cotswold landscape, the villages, and the churches. As she spoke I remembered many occasions in the past which demonstrated her love for the town and the affection that its inhabitants feel for her.

During her early seasons at the theatre she was a familiar and friendly figure as she carried a neat little shopping basket in expeditions along the High Street. I remember visiting her in the tiny cottage on Chapel Lane, close to the theatre, where she lived with her mother, the splendid Olave. I even – and this is not something she knows about yet, forty years later – remember shyly and anonymously stuffing a bunch of lilies of the valley through her letter-box one May morning. I remember hearing of the occasion when she formally opened the new swimming pool at the grammar school and, having performed the official ceremony, disrobed to reveal a swimming costume, and dived in. I remember, one afternoon when I was sitting in the headmaster's garden, hearing her from the other side of the wall as she walked along Chapel Lane with her young niece, teaching her to sing 'The lark in the clear air'. I remember when I had invited her to speak at the Shakespeare Institute to a small group of students from the University of Montpellier. She was, she said, so nervous about doing so that she brought along Richard Pasco and Barbara Leigh-Hunt to give moral support. I remember dinners with her and Mike in the French restaurant, long since closed, including one when she pooh-poohed our prediction that she would become a Dame before long. (She did.) I remember when she and Mike came for dinner with me in a little flat I had rented for a term of sabbatical leave, and how she said she had wonderful news about the next part she would be playing, and I guessed Rosalind? Cressida? and she said, 'No, Mama Rabbit *and* First Fieldmouse' in *Toad of Toad Hall.* That was the production in which Mike was so adorable as Mole.

I remember Finty's christening, at which Judi and Mike had done me the honour of inviting me to be a godparent, thinking, I suspect (as was natural at the time – I married late), that I was unlikely to have children of my own. Later I remember visiting the whole extended family at Charlecote, when little Finty told me that her guinea pig had died but had gone to heaven, which was a great relief to us all. And there was Finty's imaginary husband, Dr David Curtains, to whom Judi frequently had to answer the door. And I remember the gloomy occasion when I went behind the scenes following a performance of Trevor Nunn's production of *Macbeth* in the main house. In The Other Place, with Ian McKellen as Macbeth and Judi as Lady Macbeth, it had been a triumph. Transferred to the big stage to fill a gap in the schedule, it was a disaster. Simple design and monochrome costumes that had looked fine within the dark walls of the studio theatre now seemed mean. Whispered speeches which had pierced the audience in the small space dwindled into inaudibility in their effort to wheedle their way across the proscenium arch. In the Green Room, the actors lay slumped in dejection. 'I'll take you out to dinner to cheer you up,' I said, and we sloped off to the Italian restaurant and had a jolly time.

There are later memories too. Of Judi and Mike presiding over the opening of the newly presented Shakespeare's Birthplace, and of Mike, thin and enfeebled by his cancer, looking desperately ill, and both of them as always putting a brave face on it, and Judi telling me as they left that he was off to see his solicitor to revise his will. And even after that, when Judi was to be awarded a prize at the annual Shakespeare's Birthday lunch, as we left the church on the way to the marquee Mike pointed to the wall separating the churchyard from the theatre gardens and said that he and Judi used to hop over that to do their courting. And we sat together, and Mike was thinner and weaker still but brave and funny and proud as ever of Judi, and she spoke Rosalind's epilogue to *As You Like It* by way of thank you for her award, and as we left after the speeches had dragged themselves out she bought us all ice creams from the van parked outside the gates of the theatre gardens. And then the bleak day when Mike was brought for burial to Charlecote, and Judi followed the coffin to the grave beside those of Mike's father and mother and her own mother, and a young actor friend of Mike's wept as he read 'Let me not to the marriage of true minds', and we threw soil onto the coffin before it was covered over.

Judi did not talk much about her performances, nor did I interrogate her about them, but I was aware sometimes, as we chatted, perhaps over a glass of wine, that deep down a process of absorption of a role was taking place. She is a great assimilator. Stories circulate of her not reading the plays in which she is to appear, but I take them with a pinch of salt. Late in 1986 I went to London to see Mike and her in *Mr and Mrs Nobody*, Keith Waterhouse's dramatisation of *The Diary of a Nobody* by George and Weedon Grossmith. It was an enchanting performance of a delightful if slight comedy of manners. In her dressing room afterwards she told me that her next role was to be Cleopatra, and asked me about the meaning of a line in the play. Already she was mulling it over, and I have no doubt that the role grew steadily in her imagination as she pursued her daily tasks well before rehearsals began.

The fact that Judi would play two such contrasting roles at Carrie Pooter and Cleopatra in immediate succession is a measure of her range as an actress, a range displayed both in the diversity of the roles she has played and in the variety that she finds within a single role. She is a great joker, a giggler, a husky chuckler, and a hearty laugher, famous for the jokes she plays on her fellow actors, even onstage, and for corpsing. In a chapter she was kind enough to write for a book – *Shakespeare: An Illustrated Stage History*, edited by Jonathan Bate and Russell Jackson – which, rather like this one, was presented to me by friends and colleagues, she tells of a performance of *The Merchant of Venice*. It's one of her least favourite plays, and she had to wear a terrible wig.

In the casket scene Michael Williams was standing in the centre of the stage as Bassanio, about to make his choice. There was the wind band at the back of the stage, Peter Geddes as Gobbo, Polly James waiting to sing 'Tell me where is fancy bred', and my brother Jeff and Bernard Lloyd as monks. I was supposed to say:

> I speak too long, 'tis but to peize the time,
> To eke it, and to draw it out in length,
> To stay you from election,

But I said 'erection'. The band just put down their instruments and walked off, as did the monks, leaving Polly James to sing on her own. I have never been in such a state, and the scene had only just started.

This irrepressible sense of fun, the lack of self-importance that it betokens, the ability, even the desire, to laugh at herself, are among the qualities that make her a natural team player, and also, ever since she has been a star, the natural leader of any company in which she appears. But it should not be mistaken for a lack of seriousness in her approach to her art. Her understanding of what she has to say is complete; there is never a false emphasis. She has a deep sense of responsibility to her audiences, a determination not to sell them short. Throughout the interviews that she gives there runs an emphasis on the actor's need for training and especially, in performing Shakespeare, for coaching in vocal delivery and in understanding the demands of the verse. She has paid tribute to her teachers in this, among them Cicely Berry, John Barton, and Peter Hall. She rightly sees herself as the bearer of a tradition, and she can be quite fierce in talking about deficiencies in the voice training offered to young actors.

She has spoken of the need in verse speaking for legato, the quality in singing that carries the tone through over a succession of syllables. The famous huskiness of her voice, the catch in it that has so often been observed, that has been seen as a trademark, and even as a handicap – 'Judi Dench does not have a cold, this is her natural speaking voice' – and that gives the title to John Miller's book about her, is not naturally conducive to legato. She is not gifted with the 'voice beautiful' of the Terry family. Yet she can convey an impression of legato through a technical and imaginative mastery that is a result of a highly developed artistry.

Her vocal delivery is of exemplary clarity and energy, reminiscent of that of her great predecessor, Peggy Ashcroft. The voice is fully projected. The vowels are pure, the consonants crisp. Every syllable is required to make its contribution. She can speak fast if the situation demands it, but there is never an impression of haste. She is conscious of rhythm, but does not overstress it. She knows where the caesura, the break within the line, occurs, and she can use it, perhaps with a scarcely perceptible pause, a little silence, that suggests the working of the character's mind, the thought processes in which meaning and poetry coalesce. She knows where the line endings are, but can carry the sense over them if that is what is needed.

The seriousness that Judi brings to technical matters is no less apparent in her characterisation of roles. She looks for the humanising touches, the person below the style. This was true even in Trevor Nunn's musical based on *The Comedy of Errors*. The performance can be seen on video, and it is full of immensely skilled and endearing performances by, among others, Michael Williams, Roger Rees, Nickolas Grace, and Judi herself. It was rapturously received by Stratford audiences, and when it transferred to London was awarded the Society of West End Managers' Award for the best musical of 1976. I felt terribly curmudgeonly in not much liking it when I first saw it. I had recently edited the play, I felt great affection and admiration for it, I had loved Clifford Williams's entirely 'straight', but still very funny and touching production of 1962, with Alec McCowen as an incomparable Antipholus of Syracuse, and now I resented what I saw as condescension in turning the play into a musical, as if it were not a masterpiece in its own right. Also I was far more stuffy about musicals then than I am now.

When I watched the video again recently I still felt overall disappointment in its treatment of the play, but had to recognise the great technical skill that Judi brings to the role of Adriana. A high spot is the wordless interpolated moment when she appears on a balcony, impatient for her husband Antipholus to come in to dinner, and sees his identical twin brother, of whose existence she is oblivious, in the courtyard below. Drawing herself up to her full (not very great) height in a wonderfully imperious manner, like a latter-day Sarah Siddons, she glares at the hapless twin, and with a gesture like that of an exasperated traffic police-woman directs him into the house for what can only be going to be an exceedingly uncomfortable confrontation. This is splendid, but Judi knows that farce needs to be grounded in reality, and her performance succeeds in the way in which she underlies the exaggerations required by the production style with touches of true feeling that draw sympathy for Adriana in her plight.

The production style of *The Comedy of Errors* constricted the play's emotional range, which though relatively slight makes it so clearly a precursor of Shakespeare's other play about twins in search of each other and so of themselves, *Twelfth Night*. Judi played Viola in John Barton's RSC production 202 times, from October 1969 in Stratford, and later in Australia, then London, Stratford again, and finally, in 1972, in Japan. She has written of her love for this play's 'melancholy. The degrees of love that everyone is in, sometimes with themselves, sometimes with someone else in disguise – and everyone with their idea of love.' 'Shakespeare,' she says, 'takes so many textures of that emotion, and gives it so many forms.'

John Barton spoke in similar terms: 'the text contains an enormous range of emotions and moods and most productions seem to select one – farce or bitterness or romance – and empha-sise it throughout. I wanted to sound all the notes that are there.' (This is from an interview in *Plays and Players*, November 1969.) Many-texturedness is a prime quality of Judi's acting. In writing about the production a year or two after it closed, I tried to suggest something of this quality in Judi's interpretation of Viola, and about the ways in which she conveyed it through movement, gesture, facial expression and vocal inflection:

When she first appeared at court, Valentine, congratulating Cesario on the Duke's favours, disconcertingly slapped her on the bosom; moments later, when the Duke had entered, he pointed to a stool and pulled it close to him, indicating that Cesario should sit on it; she pulled it away before sitting down; he pulled it back to him. The actress's momentary flinchings, signs of nervousness that would be under-standable in a boy newly promoted to favour at court, held an extra dimension of meaning for those who knew the boy was a girl; and so a bond of complicity was entered into with the audience. Left onstage at the end of the scene, she could reveal to us her sympathetic amusement at her own situation: 'Whoe'er I woo, myself would be his wife.' There was intelligent irony as well as wistfulness in the delivery of the line, showing us Viola's independent resili-ence as well as her affectionate nature. In her next scene with the Duke, we were given an initial reminder of the true situation as he pulled her stool towards him and held on to her to prevent her moving away, but the scene was played for its full emotional power. Judi Dench spoke her lines about 'Patience on a monument' with a quietly beautiful intensity, and late in the scene there came a brilliant fusion of a comic apprehension of an irony with a sense of deep emotion. 'But died thy sister of her love, my boy?' asked Orsino. 'I am all the daughters of my father's house,/And all the brothers, too ...', replied Cesario; and a tiny pause followed by a catch in the voice took us movingly from the fictional situation of Viola speaking equivocally to conceal her own disguise, to the reality of the situation in which she genuinely believed that she had lost her brother.

A studio recording of part of the scene made by Judi many years later, in 1998, permits an analysis, however crude, of how she spoke it. The voice is fresh, every syllable clear, but there is no hint of oratory. She opens in an almost casual, story-telling mode:

VIOLA: My [*emphasis on both 'My' and 'fa-'*] father had a
daughter [*emphasis on 'daugh-'*] loved a man [*distinct pause*],/
As it might be, perhaps, were I a woman [*upward inflection, a smile in the voice, expressive of the impossibility*],/
I [*slight emphasis*] should your lordship.
ORSINO: And what's her history?
VIOLA: [*slight pause, lowering of the tone and volume*] A
blank, my lord. [*Momentary pause*] She never told
[*emphasis on 'told'*] her love,/
But let concealment, [*barely perceptible pause on the caesura*] like a worm i'th'bud, [*slight pause*]/
Feed on her damask cheek. [*Longer pause*] She pined [*the voice opens out on the vowel, pace reduces*] in thought, [*slight pause*]/
And with a green and yellow melancholy, [*pause at the end only of this and the following line, upward inflection on the last syllable*]
She sat like Patience on a monument,/
Smiling [*emphasis on 'smi-'*] at grief. [*Pause*] Was not this
[*slight pause*] love [*emphasised*] indeed?/
[*Pace picks up*] We men may say more, swear more, but
indeed / Our shows are more than will; for still we [*slightly emphasised*] prove / Much in our vows, but little in our
love. [*Emphasis points the antithesis of 'vows' and 'love'*]
ORSINO: But died thy sister of her love, my boy?
VIOLA: I am all the daughters of my father's house, [*pause at the end only of this line*] / And all the brothers too;
[*pause; volume reduces, last words whispered as if to herself*]
and yet I know not.

This analysis, crude though it is, may help to demonstrate something of the technical basis of Judi's speaking, showing the use she can make of her awareness of the way the verse works, of how observance of line endings, of caesuras (when they exist), and of antithesis (on which John Barton, very rightly, never tires of insisting) can help the performer to release the full emotional and intellectual potential of the lines.

When Judi came to play Beatrice in John Barton's 1976 *Much Ado About Nothing*, also for the RSC, she softened the character's asperities by picking up on the suggestions in the text that Beatrice and Benedick had had a love affair in the past. The key line comes in response to Don Pedro's words, 'Come, lady, come, you have lost the heart of Signor Benedick.' 'Indeed, my lord,' she replies, 'he lent it me a while, and I gave him use for it, a double heart for his single one. Marry, once before he won it of me, with false dice.' When I mentioned to Judi that the line was often omitted, she replied that she had agreed to take the role only on condition that it was retained. It was part and parcel of her portrayal of Beatrice as a woman of some maturity, of a wisdom born of not entirely happy experience.

There was enormous fun in her performance – the slightly bawdy comedy of the scene (Act Three, Scene Four) with her girl friends, in which she has a cold, was as funny as I have ever seen it – but the ground bass of seriousness had been sounded again at the end of the second deception scene, when she emerges from hiding after hearing herself criticised. 'What fire is in mine ears?' she says. 'Can this be true? / Stand I condemned for pride and scorn so much?' I have heard the speech spoken farcically, but Judi knew better than this. It is written in the form of an abbreviated sonnet, and in responding to its lyrical style, Judi, with a tenderness that did not deny an element of self-mockery, nevertheless showed that this is a response to a learning experience, that Beatrice is a wiser woman at the end of the scene than she had been at its beginning.

For all the emphasis that Judi herself, as well as those who write about her acting, have placed on her mastery of the speaking of both verse and prose, she is a mistress too of body language. I felt this in her performance of Perdita in Trevor Nunn's production of *The Winter's Tale*. She has often teased me about my reaction to the hippy style and music of the pastoral scenes. 'It was a wonderfully exciting production,' she wrote, 'and when it came to Bohemia we all suddenly burst out into a wonderful hippy world. Not everybody liked it. I don't usually notice individual members of the audience, but I distinctly remember seeing Stanley Wells in the stalls on the first night. He had a beatific smile through the first half, but when we came to Bohemia he sat scowling.' Oh dear! I can't entirely deny that, but I shall never forget Judi's dancing in the pastoral scene, imbued as it was with a kind of innocent eroticism, a rapt enjoyment of the music and of the sensuous movement of her own limbs that fully justified Florizel's praise:

> *When you do dance, I wish you*
> *A wave o'th'sea, that you might ever do*
> *Nothing but that, move still, still so,*
> *And own no other function.*

Body language seemed especially important too when Judi moved to the National Theatre to play Gertrude in Richard Eyre's production of *Hamlet*. I saw the play on its first night, when Daniel Day-Lewis played Hamlet – after withdrawing from the production he was succeeded by Jeremy Northam, and then by the dying Ian Charleson. In response, perhaps, to the broad dimensions of the Olivier stage and auditorium the play was performed in a presentational manner, formal rather than intimate. Characters stood far apart, and spoke often with little or no movement, facing out to the audience rather than addressing one another. The production style held the audience at arm's length, encouraging observant neutrality rather than involvement in the characters' emotions and in the excitement of the action.

Only in the closet scene between Gertrude and Hamlet did body language come into full play. As Hamlet's passion mounted he bestraddled his mother; her evident tenderness for him sought physical expression, and their climactic kiss was a naked and mutual acknowledgement of desire that shocked her. She addressed 'What shall I do?' to herself, acknowledging the discovery within herself of depths she could not fathom. As Hamlet left she collapsed, and for the rest of the play was a broken woman. Judi's acting communicated emotional complexity with great economy of means, and set the play's heart beating as it had not done until that point. I sent her a note expressing my admiration, and she telephoned to thank me for the reassurance it had given about a performance with which she was far from happy.

The Shakespeare role that gave Judi the greatest scope for the full range of her talents is Cleopatra, and she embraced its challenges and opportunities with joyous acceptance of all it has to offer, extending herself into every aspect of the role, from the sordid to the sublime, while never losing the sense of a unifying self that could encompass the character's 'infinite variety'. From her first appearance this was clearly a woman of volatile passions, physically restless, richly sensual, yet with a shrewd, instinctive intelligence that probed suspiciously, vulnerably, behind the appearances with which she was presented. She realised the comedy of the role with perfect timing and brilliant transitions. As she questioned the messenger about Octavia, her self-confidence grew until, as he said, 'I do think she's thirty,' the smile froze on her face and, gathering her skirts, she swirled abruptly around, ran towards the door, and almost left the stage.

The poetry of the role, too, was fully realised, climactically when, her restlessness subdued, she spoke 'I dream'd there was an Emperor Antony' with rapt, hushed lyricism to a Dolabella who stood in the auditorium aisle with his back to us, so that she was addressing us as well as him. The audience's silence was palpable. We were united in a single emotional response.

As everyone knows, it is difficult not to write about Judi as if one were penning a love letter. Well, what the hell. Who would want to deny her beauty, her charm, her intelligence, her kindness, her wit, her generosity, her jokiness, her compassion, quite apart from the fact that she is along with only Ellen Terry, Edith Evans and Peggy Ashcroft, one of the greatest actresses of the twentieth century and beyond? So here's another bunch of lilies of the valley for you, Judi.

A Lass Unparallel'd

MICHAEL PENNINGTON

Some people, it seems, have always been there. And when Judi Dench arrived in London as Ophelia to John Neville's Hamlet in September 1957, I was too. It was a very young debut: she was near enough my contemporary, I felt, one of us on the stage of the Old Vic and the other firmly in the pit, inflamed with enthusiasm for Shakespeare and for this theatre in particular. Because of a decision I'd already quietly made, I was, as usual, wondering how it was feeling up there: what had rehearsals been like, and these people – were they scary, were they fun, were they like me? Taken up as I was with the male models for what I one day hoped to be, such as Neville himself, I maybe didn't pay the attention I should have done to the distaff side, even though Judi's arrival had for weeks been a journalistic issue: 'London's new Ophelia – Old Vic makes her first-role star'. How few papers would that sell nowadays?

And, dotted around me, some of the critics were writing words about 'a girl called Judi Dench' that they've no doubt been eating ever since, while others, to do them justice, saw a light dawning. Myself, I registered the Ophelia as good, but I too failed to notice that I was watching a champion leaving the starting blocks.

One of the pleasures of our job is that you eventually get to meet and work with a startling number of the people you admired, even who inspired you to go into it yourself; it can happen any day, suddenly, on any project. It's not only a pleasure, but an intrinsic part of things: in a subtle way it keeps the whole organism going. Seven years later I got to Stratford, having cleared the inconvenient hurdles of school and university, and started to get back to what I'd dreamed of in the first place. Now I could answer my own question – would I belong here? It was immediately clear that if all theatre companies were like the RSC of that time, I was in for a good life, not only doing the work I loved but in a great professional community. I'm thinking of the welcome extended to the newcomer: the friendly approval as you stumble out onto your first stages; the considered warmth of your colleagues' first congratulations; the wisdom of the advice, the confidences of people who have been doing it ten times longer than you.

For me, part of this nurturing came from Michael Williams, who had not yet met Judi Dench, she having left the RSC after a first outing just as he had joined it. Michael was quite a glamorous figure, one of a small elite so in demand at the RSC that he was commuting between Stratford and London to play at both ends of the repertoire. His London job was with Peter Brook, no less, in *The Marat/Sade*, while in Stratford he was playing Dromio of Syracuse, the Painter in *Timon of Athens* and Rosencrantz in *Hamlet*. I felt that some of the glamour was rubbing off on me as I was understudying him in *Hamlet*, this being a relationship that perfectly exemplifies the welcome I'm talking about, since the encouragement and solicitude of a principal actor towards his understudy is a sign of the true professional. I felt I was now a significant part of the RSC's complex business; the trains never let us down, so I never went on for him, but I felt good.

By the time I got back to Stratford in 1976, Michael, though not in the fashion of those days an obvious romantic, had turned a number of Shakespeare's heroes – Orlando, Troilus – into himself, as well as a couple of anti-heroes – Petruchio and Bassanio. Things were looking up: such parts were now being cast by temperament rather than a classical profile. Also, he had met and married Judi, and one of the theatre's great love stories was under way, marked not only by the joy of Finty's birth, but in due course (did I say not an obvious romantic?) by his gift to her of a rose every Friday.

Before she met Michael, Judi had, I think, lived in a cottage opposite the theatre, in Chapel Lane, where she cooked up her Viola and Hermione; now three generations of them – to include her mother and Michael's parents as well as Finty – were out among the deer at Charlecote Park, while I lived in the same cottage at Chapel Lane, forever associating my parts that season with wood spiders, Russian vine and the two wonderfully crested Muscovy ducks that used to sit on the front step.

So it was that I met Judi at last, though initially more in the Green Room than on the stage; and the warmth of her greeting reminded me of the welcome Michael had extended eleven years earlier. She and he typified a remarkable company assembled that year by Trevor Nunn and John Barton, which, let's not be squeamish, has become something of a legend. Even without the glow of hindsight, most people would say that it was quite a harvest: an astute mix of established and breaking stars, a classical ensemble that seemed able to do anything – and not only the classics, as the work at The Other Place and The Warehouse in London opened out. It was a group that, though it hasn't formally stayed together, has remained an unofficial fellowship ever since, still falling into each other's arms at unlikely times, with cries of 'Why not again?'

When a company of actors is that well matched they generate a trust and appetite far greater than the sum of their parts. Though I still didn't know her specially well, I found myself urging Judi, who was already playing three leads in the season, to offer to take on Regan in *King Lear* as well. It's hardly a star part, she certainly didn't need it, but much to the delight of all concerned, she thought she would. It would come hot on the heels of *Macbeth*, instead of an entirely deserved rest. In the event my bright interfering idea was to be a fine performance that, for reasons none of us could fathom, she was ashamed of, so that she withdrew from it as soon as she was contractually able. For her the season had really ended with that magnificent Lady Macbeth.

Who's Best is a mug's game – which was the best performance, the greatest acting – it depends which night, for one thing; but it's been hard ever since to match what Judi did in that legendary *Macbeth*, which turned the season into a great one and has perhaps affected the play for good. She was completely terrifying. You felt there was a constant whispering in her ears, that something gibbered at her shoulder, that she glimpsed the heart of evil among the shadows. She somehow seemed to become younger as she became sicker and more sleepless; and her sightless gaze in the shattering sleepwalking scene showed the whole cost. Completely undisguised, just Judi in that black dress and head-scarf, not a trace of her seemed to be there; she had been filled up by this harrowed woman, aching with the poison in her veins. Well, you just don't see acting like it.

She and I first got married not long after, in 1978, in *The Way of the World*, by pure chance really, since another show had had to be cancelled and it was rushed in. Some substitute. Judi was born to play the Millamant of a thousand admirers, 'her fan spread and her streamers out, and a shoal of fools for tenders', while, stalking her as 'sententious' Mirabell, I tried to get her to 'dwindle into a wife' while trying not to dwindle beside her as a performer. It was the first thing of that size I'd done at the RSC and I'd never been opposite anyone of that power before. I rapidly learned all about raising your game. It was a little like trying to play championship tennis with the aim not of winning but of ending up equal – playing for an infinite tie-break, you might say. And of course Millamant, all champagne and light, turned into Judi, just as Lady Macbeth, in her restless ecstasy, had done. To anyone who knows or has watched her, I don't need to describe the bubble that lay under:

MIRABELL: *You are merry, madam, but I would persuade you for a moment to be serious.*
MILLAMANT: *What, with that face?*

or the sexiness beneath her marriage terms:

MILLAMANT: *Positively, Mirabell, I'll lie a-bed in a morning as long as I please.*
MIRABELL: *Then I'll get up in the morning as early as I please.*
MILLAMANT: *Ah! Idle creature, get up when you will . . .*

or how she did 'I *hate* your *odious* provisoes' with, it seemed, quite the opposite meaning in mind.

Such was our hard-headed engagement; by the time Judi met her serial husband again, in Peter Shaffer's *The Gift of the Gorgon*, fifteen years had gone by. Apart from everything else, she was the Dame. *A Fine Romance* with Michael had been and gone, and she was in the midst of *As Time Goes By*, while shuttling with me between ancient Thebes, Santorini and Enniskillen, locked in a monstrous struggle between Athena and Perseus, Christian mercy and pagan retribution, in a playful courtship that ended in the most spectacular violence. It was, by an ancient law of theatre, such a brutal journey that my main memory is of hilarity. Certainly I would never dream of horsing about with anyone else as I do with Judi: with her, the games are inseparable from best efforts. They're a way of breathing under pressure; they allow her to go on clean, ready instantly to use whatever you do onstage and to give you back something new to match it. She is always alive, a fish in her natural water.

Amy's View, her first James Bond, *Mrs Brown, Shakespeare in Love* . . . Remarried in 1998 and none the worse for wear, we found a delightful point of rest in Eduardo di Filippo's *Filumena*. If Millamant is Mirabell's victim, and the honours are even between the Damsons in *Gorgon*, Domenico Soriano is the prey

of Filumena, impotently pursuing the truth of which of her three
sons is his; she never tells him, on the basis that he will then
favour one over the others. This would be a bad bargain: she has
gone to the trouble of getting him to marry her and legitimise
all three by feigning imminent death. This is the most wonderful
play, worldly without cynicism and full of sentiment without
mawkishness, an hilarious mockery of Neapolitan *machismo*.
Filumena triumphs as all Domenico's paternity fingerprintings
fail: he was a singer, but all three boys are tone-deaf; conversely,
he was a ladies' man but all three of them are as well. The first
night was shaky, as we both know, but the show was a hit and a
boundless pleasure, like swimming every day in warm waters:

> DOMENICO: *Tell me, which one is my son, my flesh, my blood?*
> *... You can't imagine what's in here, the pain in my heart*
> *... Look, I can't breathe. See. It won't go in.*
> *[She listens to his breathing. It seems to be fine.]*
> FILUMENA: *Oh well, all right ... It's the plumber.*
> DOMENICO: *He's a good lad. Yes, of course, the plumber ...*
> FILUMENA: *It's Riccardo.*
> DOMENICO: *The shirtmaker?*
> FILUMENA: *No. It's Umberto, the writer ... Now listen care-*
> *fully, Dummi ... I loved you all my life, with all my heart.*

One night Judi said, I don't remember being so *contented* on
a stage as at this moment in Act Three, when husband and wife
sit and gently settle their scores. Well, me neither, said I; by this
time I felt I'd known Judi as long as Domenico had Filumena.
There may be bigger nights in the theatre, huger demands on
the actor, but to know a colleague so well you can read a flick of
their brow or their tiniest hesitation is a form of heaven.

There's always been a mystery about someone this good – for the
public, and for us as well. How does she do it, the critics say,
delighted not to be able to work it out. How can anyone so

playful grip your heart so effortlessly? Answer, because she's never lost her childhood faith. Who would have thought someone so self-mocking could inspire an entire profession? Judi Dench is a player, that better word for an actor, and, for all her ferocious self-criticism, the glee she finds in the sport never seems to leave her. The job gets done like a playground conspiracy: her mischief is a way of linking the dressing room and the stage, of not losing an essential childishness on her way along the corridor.

As part of this, there is, with her, a private network of ongoing narratives, conducted with all the intimacy of secret liaisons. One has to do with the Black Glove, but that is really between her and Tim Pigott-Smith. But she and I know about the Flying Fruit Salad, and we also know about Mouse Murders. Then there is the matter of the Plums. Having been Mirabell, and then Edward Damson with her, you can see how it is that we became Mr and Mrs Plum to each other; and how it is that successive birthdays have rung an infinite number of variations on the theme, though I thought the plumber's wrench was a bit much.

The jokes are also her reward for the tremendous gift she gives her audience. When I said she has always been there, I meant more than a conceit. She defies the theatre's short memory: anyone who saw her Lady Macbeth or Cleopatra, her Beatrice, Titania or Lady Bracknell, is unlikely to forget it. She also blinds you to the past for a moment like a flash-bulb, eclipsing her predecessors; once she plays a part, it stays played, you might say. But her talent is essentially generous and progressive, implicitly inclusive; in due course you find yourself thinking, well, that was a great earlier performance, and it still is, but then there was Judi. In the same way, I suspect the memory of what she's done is more often an inspiration for her successors than a terror. In her world, everyone gets their due; she is the first among equals.

For this is, like her Cleopatra, a lass unparallel'd. For one thing, it's the generosity: something in her acting taps into a vein that leads straight to the heart. It's also the speed: she can move from a thought to a related half-thought, complicate it with a burst of feeling and move on to a physical action that incorporates all three, like mercury, at the speed of light. All great Shakespearians are quick – look at Gielgud: mind and tongue simultaneous. Her sense of humour lurks even under her most intense performances, and you see that the energy that makes her laugh comes from exactly the same place as where she creates her most painful work. Thus it is that she can knit and giggle and then stand up and play Regan; in fact it's necessary for her to knit in order to play Regan. When she is, as she was in that, occasionally unhappy, it is difficult often to understand quite why. Judi's response to atmosphere is like that of a cat.

It's an open secret that, though we enjoyed ourselves, she didn't really find *The Gift of the Gorgon* congenial. It's been suggested that it was because of its interest in a most unChristian revenge, but her part represented the opposition to that; it might have been the play's form, a simultaneous weaving of past and present, but that is a technical matter that could give her, of all people, no trouble at all. In fact both theories underrate her. The real reason for her occasional unhappinesses is deep and undefined, even perhaps by herself. Something in it was wrong for her, something, she didn't know what, just didn't work. You might as well ask a cat why it bristles.

Judi used to talk of Shakespeare as the Gentleman Who Pays the Rent – well, only just, I'd say, and how good that she's found another way of doing that. Watching this latter film career, the one that makes everyone smile to see, you realise she is gathering the same reward that came to Peggy Ashcroft, who also played everything from Juliet to the Countess in *All's Well That Ends Well* and then found a huge new audience in movies as if she were starting all over again without the painful bits. It's a good comparison. The two of them (and Paul Scofield too) are among the very few with that perceptible moral authority, the implicit virtue the public seeks from artists; it is magnetised by her not only because of her work but by some sense that she is a force for good. So they flock to her as they do to very few, truly loving her in a way that actors, however admired, rarely are. As her friends, we ask her not to wear herself out by answering *every* letter, by seeing every caller, but it's hopeless; she always will, it is the right thing to do, and her faith – her original faith and her faith in her profession – makes it compulsory.

Her friendship is one of life's enriching certainties. Her loyalty is heroic; her generosity like a thermal spring. Her bullshit detection includes you; her laughter is arterial. Her prejudice in your favour can be magnificently blind, as ferocious as her requirement that you look her in the eye if she is not sure what exactly you are up to. The riot of conversation around her has been known, as in John Gielgud's centenary Gala, to be heard onstage. But when Michael died three years ago it was somehow silenced. His had been a mighty battle, eighteen months in which despair and calm alternated without quite turning into hope, as each month he rose a little then fell a little more.

On a crisp bright wintry day we came to the funeral, intent, aghast; some from New York, some from just down the road; some who had been close at hand, others who had stood beyond the perimeter fence surrounding this terrible event. Trevor Nunn spoke, surpassingly; Judi wore a defiant red. Sammy Williams, at three and a half, looked miraculously like his grandfather. Afterwards, in the white dazzle, Judi threw a party, as if a party was what was expected of her; as if we wouldn't, any one of us, have done it for her. Beneath the oil portrait of Michael sitting in his chair (just above where he would have been sitting in his chair) we all shouted and kissed each other; while in the rooms off there was quiet, as if they were side chapels in which we thought about what had happened, about how, as for Othello, it should be now 'a huge eclipse of sun and moon'. What would happen when we left? What of the next years, since the word, whenever things had gone wrong, had always been that she wanted 'to go home to Michael'. You might as well cut a person in half, it seemed, as take him from her.

But of course, she has survived, inspirationally. *Iris, Chocolat,*

The Shipping News, more Bond . . . I'm still waiting for our fourth marriage. Meanwhile, I have her plum tree in my garden, and I'm looking at it as I write. There was a little difficulty when she sent it last birthday, and, mistaking its hardy nature, I thought it might not survive the winter. But it has attended to itself; it's found strength in its depths, and now it's coming into blossom again. Dear Mrs Plum, I hope you always will.

On a Roar

TREVOR NUNN

The group investigating the text of *The Comedy of Errors* in the main rehearsal room of the Royal Shakespeare Company was very concentrated; early play, regular verse, punctuation at the end of the pentameter line ... strange high-pitched noise, persistent, monotonous ... frequent use of rhyme, frequent use of crude vocabulary ... high-pitched noise becoming piercing, torturous ... investigation of text stopped and investigation of noise began. The circle of actors became a posse, ears pressed to walls, radiators, floorboards, light fittings, public address speakers. But no source could they find.

A few minutes later, we re-assembled in our circle and picked up our texts again, frustrated that nobody had located the noise but happy that it had stopped. So where were we? Ah, yes ... the rhyming is often key to the comic effect, which is why the preceding rhyme word must be offered emphatically and ... the noise came back. What was it – a drill used for root canals, or brain surgery, or to dig up roads in the fairy kingdom? Whatever it was, it beat Chinese water torture in its devastating ability to penetrate the pain threshold.

It was when it broke up the rehearsal for the third time that I noticed my leading lady was less vocal, less palpably frustrated than the rest of the group. Judi Dench seemed to have a tight-lipped, somewhat pursed reaction in contrast to the moans and shouts all around her. I caught her eye. She exploded in convulsive laughter. The noise stopped. Then she confessed. She and she alone was the source and fountainhead of the disruption – an incredibly high-pitched hum she can keep going for minutes on end with the expertise of a great ventriloquist. 'Do it again,' everybody begged, returning from their third wild goose chase delighted to discover they had become the comprehensive victims of this notorious practical joker. Coffee break and company joy.

And wherefore do I tell you this? I suppose because that minor incident represents something close to the heart of Judi as I know her. She had recently triumphed as Beatrice in John Barton's matchless 'Raj' production of *Much Ado About Nothing*, and she had even more recently become what many people still think of as the greatest of Lady Macbeths. So right at the top of the tree, she was both Stratford's head prefect and victor ludorum. But at that moment of company hilarity, she was also the naughty little sister, the joker at the back of the class, the mischief-maker that every teacher fears and every classroom worships.

Of course such behaviour doesn't quite chime with the concept of 'Dame' and the establishment aura that goes with high honours; but the simple fact is that our most revered classical actress loves a laugh. Indeed, I would say she feels she can't deliver her best unless she is having a laugh. Don't get me wrong. I am not saying she doesn't take her work seriously. She does, consumingly so. But I believe she can't bear the thought of taking *herself* seriously, and by that route, of getting things out of proportion, or the people around her getting things out of proportion. The Yorkshire in Judi, and the Irish she got from Olave, her mum, makes her insist that her feet stay on the ground however much her imagination is in the clouds.

Well, yes, you will say, but it's not that surprising to yearn for a light-hearted atmosphere when you are doing a comedy, be it Shakespeare or sitcom. But Judi is the same rehearsing Lady Macbeth, or Hermione on trial for her life in *The Winter's Tale*, or Juno grieving for her lost child in O'Casey's masterpiece; the same outlet is necessary before her imagination will go to the darkest places of the suffering human mind. As we know, she does go to these places, she returns with astonishing insights and her daring at the extremes of the psyche creates indelible impressions. But as we around her weep, she will find something to set her and the rest of 'the table on a roar'.

There are, I fear, far worse examples of her mischief than the one behind the curtain I have lifted. She has been known to nominate a small object which must be passed covertly from actor to actor, from hand to hand, during the course of a performance. If you receive it, you must not blench, nor must you betray to the audience the moment at which you pass it on to the next unfortunate colleague. The cast of one of Judi's triumphs became so devoted to her challenge of passing a glove to each other during the run of their show that when performances of that play finished, they went on organising that it must be passed among them even though they were doing different plays in different parts of the country. Any of them doing a first night in the West End knew for certain sure, at some point during the evening, that glove would be pressed into their reluctant hand.

But since, as legend has it, Judi appeared on the main stage at Stratford as an unscheduled (and extremely diminutive) Cardinal in my RSC production of *Henry VIII*, I know that nothing and nowhere is off limits for the joker. Most recently, she arrived on the barricades of my production of *Les Misérables* as a white-bonneted, poor Parisian woman, proudly wearing her Tricolor sash as she sang her heart out in support of the revolution. The unsuspecting audience in the Queen's Theatre had no idea that this fervent woman was simultaneously playing the Countess of Rossillion in *All's Well That Ends Well* in the Gielgud Theatre next door on Shaftesbury Avenue. The Countess she re-assumed a few moments later was, of course, as wise and beatific as she had always been. So much did Judi love her mid-show metamorphosis that she was instantly planning to turn up in a few other West End productions within dashing distance. Her fellow actors love her for her, what shall I call it? – disestablishmentarianism – and it's not often one gets to use *that* word.

Her reputation among actors goes before her, and so, as I have claimed many times before, if Judi is in your acting company the job of creating an ensemble is already three-quarters done. She is available to everybody, passionate about the young, concerned for those in difficulty, exemplary in her dedication, inspirational in her work, and wickedly, ceaselessly, joyously funny.

Judi laughs at herself too, perhaps because she is extraordinarily accident-prone. I was strolling down Waterside at Stratford with her, chatting about *Macbeth* (as one does), when suddenly I realised she had disappeared. I looked all around and discovered to my consternation that she was lying stretched out on the pavement. I rushed back to her to help the fallen, but she jumped up before I could get to her. 'It's all right,' she laughed, 'I'm always falling down ... you'll get used to it.' Since then I have seen her stumble alarmingly many times, but never again that full-length dive into the gutter. Well, except once perhaps, but that's another story ...

Accidents come in many forms, not all of them attributable to bad balance. Judi and I went together once to the annual Stratford-upon-Avon Mayoral Reception for the RSC, when we were introduced to the delightful and articulate Mayor, a man whose achievements were all the more remarkable because he was blind. I don't know what fatal magnet led Judi to describe the recent redecoration of the main Stratford theatre auditorium to the Mayor, but when she capped her enthusiasm with 'Just wait until you see it ... you'll be ... oh, I mean ...', our little group went very quiet as, it seemed for thirty seconds, nobody could think of anything to say.

Ripple dissolve to a week later, when Judi and I were walking, in the evening, through the main Stratford thoroughfare towards a restaurant. We were hailed from the other side of the street and realised the Mayoress was beckoning to us, explaining to her husband that we were crossing to greet them. I just had time to whisper to Judi, 'Remember, don't talk about *seeing* things,' and there we were. 'Oh, Mr Mayor,' said a breathlessly convivial Judi, 'how wonderful to hear you again!' The next five minutes were almost unbearable. I knew if I caught Judi's eye, we would both become a disgrace to our profession. I could sense her gasping and gagging to suck the unwanted laughter back into her windpipe, so that only isolated hiccups distorted the odd word in each sentence she spoke.

When we were on our own again I watched her sob with laughter, her face desperately unwilling to laugh at what had just happened, but racked with unstoppable tears of mirth that washed away every scrap of make-up. Judi's laughter is terribly contagious, irrefutable, irresistible – and redemptive in its innocence. It springs from her sense of the postures and fronts that we all have, that we use for our work and for our lives, and how effortlessly they can be demolished, or will farcically implode when touched. But she has that sense about herself most of all.

She told me once that, at all the moments of recognition and achievement in her life, she is sure to be tapped on the shoulder by a little man whose sole function, exactly on cue, is to dump a metaphorical bucket of water over her. Best of all is her story of the local dignitary in Haringey, who was a very unlikely man to be carrying that bucket. The occasion was the official ribbon-cutting ceremony to open the Judi Dench Theatre that had been built in the borough. Judi had been immensely flattered that a drama school, erecting its own new theatre, should have asked if they could use her name for their building.

She stood waiting to cut the ribbon, as the dignitary launched into his encomium on their illustrious guest – 'who needs no further introduction, star of stage and screen, who has given her name to our theatre, ladies and gentlemen, Miss Judy Geeson'. Splosh. But, you see, the only reason that I know this story is because Judi tells it herself, she punctures her own balloon, she places her own banana skin, and refuses to personify the dignity that she senses is required of her.

Alas, there was one dreadful occasion when I thought Judi was joking and she wasn't. It was that other occasion when she fell inexplicably to the ground. She had been the life and soul of the rehearsals of a risky, somewhat experimental musical project by Andrew Lloyd Webber called *Cats*. She had danced and sung, and bravely led the improvisational work I had set up by her dauntless example. One day, as my colleagues and I chatted during a brief break, Judi was crossing the rehearsal room floor when she collapsed just as suddenly and inexplicably as she had that day in Waterside. I was entirely confident that she was about to leap up again with a self-deprecating laugh. But this time it was for real. The paramedics told me, as she was taken away to hospital, that she had snapped an Achilles tendon, or as somebody in the company whispered as our spiritual leader was carried away, 'It's almost as bad as breaking your leg.' So it proved. Judi never opened in *Cats*, despite her formidable determination to return to the show, in plaster and in pain.

Many people have asked me how her version of 'Memory', the hit song from the show, would have been received. In reply I have to tell you yet another tale. Two weeks after her injury, and still set on rejoining the cast before our opening, Judi came one night to rehearse the song with me after everybody else in the company had gone home. By then, we were working on the stage of Her Majesty's Theatre in the Haymarket, the very stage which had first revealed the miracle of *West Side Story* to the British theatre-going public. She was brought by car from a nursing home, with one leg completely encased in plaster, and was carried by her driver into the theatre. She sat on a solitary chair on the dimly lit stage and, together with a pianist in the pit, we resolved many issues about the song's musical requirements and I talked to her about the lyric I had written.

As she listened and worked, I could sense the pain she was feeling, and even more the unmistakable vulnerability and emotional frailty of the invalid. But, despite all this, we agreed it was time for her to have a go at the song. What happened as I sat, the solitary member of the audience, in that dark and ghostly auditorium was utterly unforgettable. Many artists, primarily

Elaine Paige and Barbra Streisand, have made wonderful recordings of the song and many have given brilliant performances of the role of Grizabella. But what Judi did on that strange and unverifiable occasion was of overwhelming and matchless emotional impact – plaintive, angry, brave, fearful, desperate, transcendent and yes, again, redemptive. She was in tears as much as I by the end, and as I climbed back onto the stage to confirm to her the miraculous thing that had just taken place, she sniffled and said, 'Well, that was dreadful.'

I must invade her privacy no more. Several times watching her perform I have understood why we need the term 'great acting'. She has that capacity to open herself and become a conduit for all our emotions and experiences and memories. We become unable to withhold ourselves from her. Nobody can be a great actor without being a great person, and Judi confirms this truth. Her generosity in giving of her time and her art for countless causes is the same generosity that makes us identify with her in performance. The word isn't selflessness, because she is so potently a guardian of ideals and values, in her work and her life, that underline her certainties. The word is genius, in all its contradictions, complexity and fundamental humanity. Yes, genius, and something else, a ... I'm sorry to break off, but can you hear a strange high-pitched noise?

Meaning Every Word

BOB LARBEY

$\mathcal{I}$'ve only had writer's block once in my career and I blame it on Judi Dench.

I'd submitted an idea for a situation comedy to Humphrey Barclay at London Weekend Television. It was about awkward middle-aged love and I called it *A Fine Romance*. Humphrey liked it enough to commission a pilot script. I wrote the script and, to my delight, a series was commissioned. Then came the always tricky job of casting and this is where the writer's block came in.

Humphrey had proposed that Judi's husband, Michael Williams, would be perfect as Mike – a brilliant choice – but casting Laura was proving more difficult. My wife, Trisha, had suggested Judi Dench to me but we both had grave doubts that one of the country's truly great actresses would ever consider doing a situation comedy. A little later, Humphrey and I were sitting in his office exchanging lists and getting nowhere when Humphrey asked me in a perfect world who would I cast as Laura? 'Well,' I said, 'Judi Dench,' still thinking this was about as likely as England ever winning the Ashes. But Humphrey was made of sterner stuff and said there was no harm in sending her a script – she could only say no.

A few days later, Humphrey phoned me with the news that Judi had said yes! I put the phone down in a state of shock and set about writing the remaining scripts. I thought about Judi Dench actually saying my lines and couldn't write a word for three weeks! I have since forgiven Judi.

I don't know what I expected at the read-through – a grand entrance, a fanfare, possibly a red carpet? What I got was a quiet, unfussy entrance which I later learned was typical of Judi. I demonstrated my relief by spilling coffee all over the rehearsal table.

We were lucky to get James Cellan-Jones to direct. James had been Head of Plays at the BBC and had never directed a situation comedy before, so brought no tricks with him. Judi and Michael hadn't done situation comedy before either so, as Judi said, 'just acted it'. My, how they acted it – beautifully.

Judi is the most instinctive actress I've ever worked with. In rehearsal, she would make everybody laugh or cry with some little gesture or a catch in her voice. When asked to keep it in for the performance, she often swore that she couldn't remember what she'd done. I'd expected quite a lot of suggested line changes but no. The nearest I ever remember Judi coming to that was when she once suggested, very gently, that she might be able to replace a line with just a look. Needless to say, the look was far better than the line.

The press received *A Fine Romance* well, except for one really vitriolic review based, it seemed, on the writer's belief that Judi had somehow betrayed herself by descending to the depths of sit-com. Lashing out in all directions, he even accused Susan Penhaligon, who played Judi's younger sister, of looking over-weight! Judi's response? At the next read-through, she said to Susan, 'Come on, let's have the fatties sitting together.' Judi laughed, Susan laughed, and everybody laughed. I just wish that self-important critic had been there to see it. I also hope he was there to see when the show was later awarded the Broadcasting Press Guild Award and Judi a BAFTA.

Actually, it's a common misconception among the snobbier elements in the profession that situation comedy is easy to do. It's not. It's a week's rehearsal, then into a studio for one day to record a show in front of a live audience. The only time I ever saw Richard Briers lose his temper was when we were in the

BBC Club after recording *The Good Life.* An actor of no note whatsoever breezed in after doing his two lines in a drama and said, 'Hello, Dickie, I see you've finished your little thing.' Richard told him exactly what the 'little thing' involved. A lovely moment! Judi never treated situation comedy as another piece of work. She never patronised it for one moment. In fact, shortly before the first recording, she told me she was terrified.

The first series of *A Fine Romance* ended on a high note. Indeed, before the last recording, London Weekend wanted some more. Humphrey and I talked with Judi about it and this great actress, unsteeped in the ways of television series, suggested that perhaps we should do two more. She meant two more episodes! Happily, Humphrey was able to explain that it didn't really work that way and we went on to make four series before deciding that we should go out on top.

I think and certainly hope that Judi enjoyed herself. I do know that she got a great deal of pleasure from doing something that was watched by millions and getting big bags of fan letters. She did tell me a story which showed the price of television fame though. She and Michael were in the back of a car on the way to rehearsal, not speaking because they'd had a tiff over breakfast. A taxi pulled alongside at some traffic lights and, recognising the two rather stony faces, the driver sang 'A fine romance'. A happy ending – it made Judi and Michael laugh and the tiff was over.

Rehearsals were always fun. There has to be a lead to make them so and the lead was Judi. She loves to laugh and when she laughs it's very infectious. She did provide one by doing something which wasn't intentionally funny. We were rehearsing in a big old church near Waterloo station. Of course, the altar was screened off but a rather pompous and obviously disapproving verger skulked about wearing a suspicious look instead of a smile. Judi went to the loo and had a little sing to herself. What did she sing? 'There's no business like show business!' The aforementioned verger heard her and had the nerve to tell Judi off for singing in God's house. I didn't hear Judi's reply but suffice to say that he went very quiet and lurked a good deal less after that.

Judi will always claim that she can't sing, but if you saw her onstage in *Cabaret* you'll know what she can do with a song. As a matter of fact, Judi was to play Grizabella in *Cats*, but injured her Achilles tendon whilst rehearsing a dance and had to withdraw. What a pity. I'd have loved to hear her sing 'Memory'. Much later, I heard her sing 'Send in the clowns' in *A Little Night Music* and there wasn't a dry eye in the house.

It was sad when *A Fine Romance* came to an end, but, as I said, we decided it was right to get out on top. The series had been a great success but the last episode had Mike and Laura finally realising they were in love and deciding to get married, so where was there to go? The series had been a joy to do and that's not a show-biz cliché but the truth. One thing I knew for sure, I'd never get writer's block again!

Well, I'd worked with Judi Dench and it had been a special time. I certainly didn't expect it to happen again but, happily, I was wrong. Meanwhile, Judi got a prize of some sort for almost everything she did – which was a lot. I did manage to get one myself, the London *Evening Standard* award for Best Comedy Play, and who made the effort to be there to present the award? It was Judi, of course. I started my bumbling acceptance speech by saying that I couldn't have been given the award by a nicer lady and I meant every word.

Several years later I was asked by the Theatre of Comedy if I'd like to pop up to London and talk over an idea. There was nothing to lose, so up to London I duly popped. Syd Lotterby was there with Geoffrey Palmer, whom I'd never met but greatly admired. They, and Martin Shute from the Theatre of Comedy, told me of an idea which they saw as a potential comedy series and asked if I would be interested. I went home with a synopsis which I read and liked a lot. It was Colin Bostock-Smith's idea. It was the tale of two young lovers at the time of the Korean War who lost touch because of a letter that went astray and by sheer chance met again forty years later.

Syd Lotterby was to direct and Geoffrey Palmer was already cast as Lionel, so to say we had a strong start is an understatement, but the character of Jean still had to be cast. A faint echo of putting *A Fine Romance* together did cross my mind but that's all. I didn't think for one moment that lightning could strike twice, but it did when I was told that a certain Judi Dench was to play Jean.

So that was the birth of *As Time Goes By* and what a healthy baby it turned out to be. Strangely, Geoffrey Palmer had never met Judi. He knew I had worked with her before and, quite naturally, asked me what she was like. Never one for long sentences I just said, 'She's lovely.' Something that Geoffrey swiftly found out for himself. The chemistry between them soon manifested itself in the most beautiful performances and, with Syd Lotterby instantly catching the tone and an excellent supporting cast, *As Time Goes By* got under way.

By this time, Judi knew that a second series would comprise a little more than two episodes but I don't think that she, or any of us, ever thought that we would end up doing more than seventy episodes, spaced out over more than ten years! After about the third series we all kept saying good-bye but, months later, we all found ourselves saying hello again in a different rehearsal room. I would never describe Judi as a masochist, so she must have enjoyed doing it. I think that everyone did. The cast became like an extended family and a very happy one at that.

Judi loves to laugh and that laugh is very infectious. This time round I discovered her love of practical jokes and one of her favourites was to get everybody back to the rehearsal room after lunch before Syd, and then all hide, so that Syd would come back to work and find nobody to work with. It never really worked – it's quite difficult for twelve or so people to hide effectively in one room – but I'll never forget the look of almost childlike joy on Judi's face as she said, 'Hide!' Once the female members of the cast had somehow steered Syd onto the subject of male sexual fantasies and Syd, eschewing the usual sexy under-wear one, confessed to a liking for black dresses with long black gloves. Confession over, Syd got back to work, presumably think-ing he'd heard the last of it – but not with Judi about. As we gathered for the next rehearsal there was a complete absence of ladies until Judi, Jenny Funnell, Moira Brooker and all the ladies from the production team swanned in, all wearing black dresses and long black gloves! Philip Bretherton took a photo which I'm sure Syd treasures.

One of the series was tinged with great sadness when Judi's husband, Michael Williams, became seriously ill. Our hearts went out to Judi and all of us were afflicted with that peculiar English fault of not really knowing what to say. We didn't have to worry. Judi accepted the awful strain she must have been under and somehow found the resource to work on and be as close as possible to her normal self. Among other things, Judi is very brave. Sadly, Michael died soon after we finished that series. Michael was a fine actor as well as a lovely man and all of the cast turned up at his memorial service.

Time went on and so did *As Time Goes By*, and Judi's career went from strength to strength with yet another string to her bow – films. If ever anyone deserved truly international recog-nition it's Judi and, my word, she got it. She even played M in the James Bond films and in one she sparred with a very grumpy admiral played by Geoffrey Palmer!

When she became a Dame – for having done far more than play M – we all greeted her at rehearsal with mock bows and curtseys and called her 'Your Damenosity'. Judi's answer was short and to the point – and just a little Anglo-Saxon. She also received her first Oscar nomination for *Mrs Brown*, but more of that anon.

Syd Lotterby managed to keep virtually the same production team together throughout those years, which made it all the more enjoyable and, to a man or woman, they all loved Judi. She was always prompt, always totally professional and always fun to work with. I did discover, however, that there is one word in the English vocabulary that she swore she could not pronounce. I must never reveal that word but honestly it's not a difficult one.

I can also claim that I directed Judi in one episode – even if it was for only one line. I thought it was a fairly simple line, but Judi, in rehearsal, said she didn't understand it. Trying to explain a line is actually very difficult. I tried to several times but without success. Finally, Judi suggested that I just say the line the way it was supposed to be delivered and she'd say it that way in performance. I did, she did and it worked, thus establishing my reputation as a director.

After all those good-byes and 'This must be the last series', it was decided that we really should make a last series of *As Time Goes By*, so we did. After the last recording, Don Taffner, the head of the Theatre of Comedy, laid on a party in the studio. It was a good party but, I have to say, a fairly muted one with an air of sadness about. Judi, however, brightened up the evening by sitting Syd Lotterby down and leading all the ladies in the show in rendering a rather sexy version of 'Nobody does it better' to him. Syd wasn't the only one to enjoy the song. I thanked Judi for the loan of her talent and she just smiled and shrugged. I really do believe that she finds praise embarrassing, though Lord knows she's had masses of it.

Trisha and I had bought Judi a present. It was a replica of a little old lady in a leopard-skin coat with a cigarette in one hand and a gin in the other. The message said, 'We hope you don't end up like this', and Judi loved it. We said our good-byes as the party started to break up, but then we saw her again in the car park as we waited for our car and Judi headed for hers with her agent, who happens to be a lady. Referring to the present of course, I called out to Judi, 'Make sure you look after that little old lady!' I believe to this day that Judi's agent thought I was referring to her and she had just had a brief encounter with a drunken and ill-mannered writer.

I said I'd come back to that Oscar nomination story. It was

for Judi's wonderful portrayal of Queen Victoria in *Mrs Brown*. We had our read-through on Monday and at home the next day I read in the newspaper of Judi's nomination. The article went on to say that Judi had actually received the news the day before, during the lunch break, whilst rehearsing *As Time Goes By*. I hadn't seen any such thing and dismissed that bit as paper-talk, but then thought back to that lunch-time. We were all in the BBC canteen, doing our best to digest the food, when Judi got a call on her mobile. She went over to a window to get a better reception, took the call, came back to the table and asked who wanted coffee. That call had been the news of her Oscar nomination and what had Dame Judi Dench done? She hadn't even mentioned it, but joined a queue at the counter to buy us all a coffee! How typical of Judi that is.

She didn't get that Oscar which, of course, she should have done, but justice was done when she won it soon after for playing another Queen, this time Elizabeth I in *Shakespeare in Love*. As well as being thrilled, I suspect that Judi was secretly tickled by the fact that she was only on the screen for eight and a half minutes. A perfect example of quality over quantity. The look she gave her courtiers when they were slow to lay down their cloaks so that she wouldn't have to walk through the mud was worth the Oscar alone.

I missed *As Time Goes By*. It had become like an annual reunion and always a happy one. Judi wrote me a sweet letter after it was all over, saying how thrilling it had been to do, which did my ego a power of good. I must have written many thousands of lines for Judi. Taking *A Fine Romance* and *As Time Goes By*, I work it out as about fifty hours' worth. Of course, William Shakespeare wrote a few lines for her as well, but he never had the pleasure of being at those first read-throughs.

Many better writers than I (and I do include Shakespeare) have written for Judi but I have the pleasure of knowing that I am the only one to have written situation comedy for her. I have to qualify that by adding 'so far', because Judi has a propensity for taking on just about anything providing she likes it. The range of roles she has tackled is quite mind-boggling and a tribute to her talent. 'Great' has become an over-used word and its meaning is diminished when applied to a pair of trainers, but when applied to Judi as an actress I believe it to be absolutely accurate. Time and time again she would enthral millions of television viewers with just a look or a little gesture. In *Romance* one of her favourite lines as Laura was 'It's just the way of things,' and the look in her eyes as she said it added a great poignancy. In *As Time Goes By* she worked out a way, as Jean, of coming in on the end of Lionel's lines when she obviously knew what he was going to say – intelligent and very successful. Instinct seems to play a large part in Judi's performance and what very good instincts she has. But to me Judi's biggest talent in performance is that as the character she always tells the truth. It may sound easy but it isn't. Some actors deliver a line extremely well without ever convincing the audience that they actually mean it. Judi always delivers a line as though she means every word, so always makes her characters totally believable. The result is that audiences really care about whoever she plays and that is true talent.

Given that in getting Judi as an actress you are getting one of the very best, you quickly discover that you are working with a quite remarkable lady. Modesty is inbuilt, all the more admirable because of her international status. Never once have I seen her be grand or patronising, just one member of a team doing a job. She's the most un-actressy actress you could meet. I've never heard her call anybody 'Love' or drop names, though the ones that crop up in ordinary chat seem to include just about everybody in the business! I mentioned Judi's reaction to praise. The time I saw it best was at a BAFTA tribute. Judi sat in the front row with her daughter Finty, listening to tribute after tribute from the great and the good, and I swear she was squirming with embarrassment. She only seemed to relax and laugh her socks off when the great and the good were taking the mickey out of her.

Kindness is one of Judi's virtues too. Time and again I have watched her rehearse scenes with actors who are just in for one episode. Now that's not an easy thing to do, let alone when you are playing a scene with a Dame, but Judi is always considerate and helpful and I could see, particularly with the younger actors, how much it meant to them. The same with the regular cast and crew too. Judi is always sensitive to other people's problems or sadnesses, so if you want a shoulder to cry on, Judi's is the shoulder.

Well, those are my experiences working in situation comedy with Judi Dench and if this chapter is all about happy memories, it's all I have. Judi may not be aware of just what she has done for situation comedy as a genre. Never treating it as a lesser form, she brought her already formidable reputation and talent to it with enthusiasm and sincerity. I wrote earlier that I must have written a few thousand words for Judi over the years, and I have to say that she graced every one of them – except for the one she can't pronounce.

Beatrice in *Much Ado About Nothing*, with Donald Sinden
as Benedick. Royal Shakespeare Company, 1976.

*'This is high comedy and no Beatrice in memory
has been more firmly based in truth.'*

With Richard Pasco and Michael Williams.

Laura in *A Fine Romance*, with Michael Williams as Mike.
London Weekend Television, 1980.

*'Judi and Michael hadn't done situation comedy before so, as Judi said,
"Just acted it." My how they acted it – beautifully.'*

Jean in *As Time Goes By*, with Geoffrey Palmer as Lionel. BBC, 1992–2002.

'The chemistry between them soon manifested itself in the most beautiful performances.'

*J*uno, with Dearbhla Molloy as Mary Boyle, in *Juno and the Paycock*.
Royal Shakespeare Company, Aldwych, 1980.

'She has no problem allowing herself to be vulnerable in front of her fellows.
This is one of the elements that makes her acting so truthful.'

$\mathcal{L}$ady Bracknell in *The Importance of Being Earnest*. National Theatre, 1982.

'A sexy, barely middle-aged matriarch.'

Barbara in *Pack of Lies*, with Michael Williams as Bob. Lyric Theatre, 1983.

*'As with all real artists, it's the animal instincts that rise up
and create those rare moments of greatness.'*

Carrie Pooter in *Mr and Mrs Nobody*, with
Michael Williams as Charles Pooter. Garrick Theatre, 1986.

'Mr and Mrs Nobody *is both a tour-de-force and
a tightrope walk for the duettists.*'

Mother Courage. Royal Shakespeare Company, 1984.

'A frowzy over-age punk waiting for something objectively awful but commercially gainful to happen.'

Cleopatra, with Anthony Hopkins as Antony.
National Theatre, 1987.

*'The Shakespeare role that gave Judi the greatest
scope for the full range of her talents.'*

A Better Chance of Lightning

BILL NIGHY

I think of Dame Judi Dench as unarmed. I mean she operates as an actress in the bravest way and arranges to arrive on-stage, as it were, defenceless. It's a way of saying that she is prepared not to resort to trickery. It's like walking to a spot where you've heard that lightning is about to strike and vowing not only that you won't flinch, but that you will attempt to turn it into something useful. It requires considerable courage and humility and there aren't, as you might have guessed, many people who have that.

She is in the habit, apparently, of not reading a play before agreeing to be in it. She has the director or writer tell her the story. She will turn up for the read-through and be hearing and speaking the play for the first time. This is as radical an approach as I have ever heard of, and I don't know of any other actor who does it. It's a way, I should imagine, of frightening yourself. A better chance of lightning.

Acting is something you do whilst having the wind up. You have to achieve everything required of you whilst being, particularly on First Nights, in a sort of altered state. Large amounts of adrenalin are pumped into your system, and how you respond is what counts. Dame Judi responds with a big and open heart, as well as, of course, her fierce intelligence, great instinct, and profound sense of what's funny. It takes real class to deny yourself the sort of defensive strategies a lot of actors employ. It is beyond most of us. Dame Judi, I feel, draws from, is loyal to, the notion of love.

If you've been fortunate enough, as I have, to be on the other end of one of her, what might be called, old-fashioned looks, you will know how it feels to turn onstage to see her looking at you with an irresistible mixture of innocence and mischief. It's one of my favourite things to remember. She has, you suspect, an outrageous imagination.

She has always been kind and gracious to me. She is a democrat and there aren't as many of those about as first we thought. She has never allowed me to feel outclassed.

Intuition or Instinct

DEARBHLA MOLLOY

We met at the single washbasin in the tiny ladies' loo. Tongue-tied, I tried to squeeze myself into invisibility against the wall, partly to give her some space to finish washing her hands and mostly because I had no idea how great actors were addressed in England. Miss Dench, I supposed, and from a respectful distance. This was not how I had imagined it would be. I had pictured us all sitting around the table on the first day, Miss Dench sitting at the top beside the director. By the manner of the introductions I would know the form. Here in the make-shift lavatory, partitioned off from the large attic space that had once been a warehouse for ripening bananas but was now a rehearsal room for the RSC, I had nothing to give me any clue. 'God, I hate the first day of rehearsals, don't you? Terrifying,' she said. I fell in love.

We were about to begin work on *Juno and the Paycock*, directed by Trevor Nunn in 1980. Jude was playing Juno. The rest of the cast was Irish, including Norman Rodway as Captain Boyle, and I was playing Mary. I had lived and worked in Ireland up to this, only joining the RSC at Stratford to play in *Shadow of a Gunman* a few months before, and had expected to return to Dublin after a pleasant summer by the Avon. But suddenly I was cast in another O'Casey play with Judi Dench, directed by Trevor Nunn, and at the Aldwych. This was well beyond my wildest dreams. Those three names together represented for me the peak of all possibilities. I felt as if I was supping with gods.

Rehearsals were intense, exhilarating, creative and great fun. Jude had a great talent for falling asleep, anywhere and any time. One day, putting his finger to his lips, Trevor Nunn led a group of us on tiptoe over to what looked like a pile of old stage curtains heaped in a corner. On top of the pile, in a small ball and fast asleep, was the Legend of British Theatre. Another day, we were all dismissed for the afternoon while Judi and Trevor worked on Juno's final speech, the last great challenge for the actor playing the part, and on the slopes of which many had plummeted. Next day I asked Trevor how the afternoon had gone. He started to laugh. 'We did fantastic work. We really made progress. And this morning she came in and said, "Just remind me what we agreed on that speech yesterday."' It was difficult to remain for long in awe of someone so human. Needless to add, when she came to doing that speech every night, she devastated the audience.

Almost twenty-five years later, the experience of that production, rehearsing and playing, still has a special quality for all of us involved with it. It was the play where Judi went from being the nation's ideal sweetheart to being its ideal mother. It also allowed her to explore and express the Irish side of her heritage and character. Her mother, Olave, who then lived with Judi and Michael and Finty, came from Dublin and was quintessentially Irish. The family had just been on holiday in Greece prior to rehearsal. One evening, examining her arms after a few days' sunbathing, Olave announced: 'If I go as brown as I'm red, I'll be black.' Worthy of O'Casey himself. In one of those inexplicable coincidences, Judi, Doreen Keogh and I discovered that our collective parents had all lived on the same very short road in Sandymount, in Dublin, and at the same time. Judi's parents were a young married couple, her father a recently qualified GP. He had been my father's family's doctor for a time, prior to the Denches moving to live in York. My eldest uncle remembered him well. Several years ago, after Olave died, I was in Dublin, and went to Sandymount to find the house the couple had lived in on Tritonville Road. I thought I might be able to bring something from the garden, a daisy perhaps, that Jude could press in memory. My grandmother's house is still there, as is Doreen's parents' old house, but the Denches' house seems to have been knocked down to make way for a wider road.

Trevor Nunn gave us all homework to do during rehearsal, quite apart from the usual learning lines and studying the text. Each actor was given a subject pertinent to the play and had to write a paper. These were to be read on a given date before everyone in the RSC involved with the production, from Assistant Stage Management to Marketing. Jude's paper was on 'Tenement Living in Dublin', mine on 'Women in Trades Unions'. I spent an eternity in the British Museum Newspaper Library in Colindale with miles of microfilm, finally getting my father to send me material from Ireland. Jude on the other hand, and with a style I hugely admired, called the Bodleian and had them send all the relevant information. An actor who had been in *Shadow of a Gunman*, Shay Gorman, was born and brought up in a tenement in Dublin alongside Brendan Behan's family. When Jude heard this she got in touch with him and augmented the dry library material with Shay's stories. Among the stories and anecdotes, he told her that, however poor a family was, they would always have a geranium on the windowsill. This became the emblem for the show. We had a geranium on the set, and the poster was a black-and-white photo of a Georgian tenement window, with a startlingly bright red geranium in a pot on the sill. As in her performances, Judi homed in on the small detail that made it most human.

Unlike other productions, we were not shown a model of the set on the first day of rehearsals. Instead, Trevor Nunn waited for a week or so and then produced it. We were all invited to describe how we imagined it would be before it was unveiled and, when we finally saw it, were asked if there was anything we felt should be changed. I think Trevor's idea, with which John Gunter was willing to concur, was that the set should be organic, a place we all recognised. The only area there was any disagreement on was the positioning of the fire. There was a suggestion that it should be downstage centre, requiring therefore an imaginary mantel. At the beginning of the play Juno has to cook a breakfast for the Captain, frying a sausage and boiling a kettle to make tea. The final decision had to be Judi's. She chose that the fireplace should be on the left of stage. She was also absolutely insistent that, poor though this household undoubtedly was, it should be spotlessly clean.

Reams have been written about Judi's wonderful Juno by people much more qualified to judge than I. She ticked off all the boxes. Her Juno was warm, bossy, funny, irritable, compassionate, proud, wise, generous, soaked in humanity – I could go on and on. When I finally came to play the part myself, twenty years later, I could still hear her voice on every line. I was so afraid of echoing her, I think a lot of my decisions in relation to the character were simply made in antithesis to hers.

During the run of this play my younger sister had a very bad accident. Aisling was nineteen and a student. Crossing the road in front of her university in Dublin, she was hit by a motorbike and her leg was severely damaged. She was in intensive care for some time, and subsequently had an operation every week to try to fit back the jigsaw pieces that had been her hips. She was in real danger of losing her leg and was in a serious condition for most of the run of the play. My brother and I, being completely impotent and desperate to do something, decided to fast each week on the day the operations took place. We hoped that by focusing our energy on our sister, as positively as possible, we might have some beneficial effect. The operating day fell on our matinée day. The canteen in the Aldwych was the size of a large cupboard, impossible to keep any eating habit secret. Judi noticed I never seemed to eat on the day of the weekday matinée, and asked me why. I told her. She announced that she too would fast for Aisling, until Aisling was better. Jude was playing a huge part, eight times a week, and fulfilling who knows how many other engagements during the daytime as well as being a wife and mother. On the toughest day, a two-show day, she never ate a bite. She sent presents and cards every few weeks, although she had never met my sister, and she, and Michael, continued to fast for Aisling for the best part of a year.

Jude's generosity is legendary and as I look around my home my eye constantly falls on objects she has given me. A beautiful rounded wooden heart, carved out of the heart of one of the oak trees in her garden felled by the huge storm of 1986. A pottery wall plate, on it the image of a cottage set between rounded hills. (She told me this was a cottage I would live in one day. As I write, I have been living in it for ten years.) But her real generosity is not in giving things, but in giving those parts of herself that are far more valuable and cost her far more. She gives time, and commitment, and passion, and loyalty, and her word. In the deepest sense of the word, what she gives is love.

Loyalty is one of the qualities Judi values the most, she once told me. Her own loyalty is unequivocal. During the run of *The Plough and the Stars*, which we did at the Young Vic, my marriage disintegrated. Jude took me under her wing like a damaged duckling, bringing me down to her house in the country, feeding me delicious tidbits like an anxious mother, and tucking me up luxuriously among feathers, linen and lace. My soon-to-be-ex husband telephoned at one point. Jude had not heard his side of things at all, but her responses to him were terrifyingly terse. Within about two seconds he got the gist of Jude's opinion of him loud and clear. To have her on your side is a wonderful thing. To have her against you is not to be imagined. It's possible to imagine her killing for those she loves. She is fearless for any person or creature under her protection. One night, she saw a mouse in her house and attempted to catch it to save it from the cats. The mouse bit her for her kindness. She had to go to hospital immediately for anti-tetanus injections.

Jude is well known for never reading scripts. Either Michael read them for her, and then told her the story, or whatever director was trying to get her to do the play. Sam Mendes very much wanted Judi to play Bessie Burgess in his production of *The Plough and the Stars* and asked if I would pitch the story for him, so to speak. I rang Jude and explained the plot as best I could. I told her that every great Irish female actor had played the part from Sara Allgood to Siobhan McKenna to Marie Kean. I began to realise I wasn't getting very far with my mission. Jude's monosyllabic responses were making me nervous. I ploughed on, getting increasingly desperate, mentioning en passant that it was not a very big part. 'Not a big part?' she interrupted. 'I'll do it.' Intuition, or instinct, connection is one of the ruling principles of her life. It determines how she chooses everything, from parts to people. When I first went to the house she used to own in Hampstead, I observed how calm and peaceful the colours were. The house was down a tiny narrow lane, facing a very old graveyard. Beneath the trees, the ancient lichen-covered headstones were randomly scattered about the daisy-and-dandelion-flecked grass. Judi said that when she bought it, before she did anything at all to the house, she had stood for a long time looking out her window at the scene opposite. As near as possible, she sketched the colours before her. Then she brought the outside in, using these colours to decorate and furnish.

Shortly after *Juno and the Paycock*, I stopped acting for several years and turned to study. After five years, I decided to return to the theatre, emboldened by an offer to play Lady Macbeth at Bristol. I think I might be the only actor in history to have spent almost three years with the Royal Shakespeare Company and never spoken a line of Shakespeare except in Terry Hands' sonnet classes. I had never played a Shakespearean character anywhere. I was terrified. Then I remembered Judi had promised to teach me the rules. She had been a groundbreaking Lady Macbeth for the RSC. In light of this, we decided to use the text for *Antony and Cleopatra*, which she was currently playing. I wrote down the rules as she gave them to me, and have carried them in my diary ever since. She said they had come down in a direct line from Ellen Terry, and I must promise to pass them on in my

turn. Here they are, in no particular order, Judi Dench's Rules of
Shakespeare:

1 Obey the metre.
2 Remember it's a play, not reality.
3 Be specific – don't generalise.
4 Start scenes.
5 Earn a pause.
6 Don't separate. Don't leave air between the sentences.
7 Drive through the speech.
8 Economy, simplicity, and negotiate with humour.
9 Play the antithesis, the pauses, and go up at the end
   of lines.
10 You don't have to carry the message, the play does it
   for you.
11 Trust the play, and your casting.
12 Don't comment on the character.

Apart from the rule about obeying the metre, and maybe the
one about going up at the end of lines, it seems to me that all
the above advice can apply to all writers, and all acting, whether
theatre, radio or film. If only being a great actor was as easy as
obeying the rules.

And while we're on recipes, here's the recipe for what became
known in our house as Jude's Pud, as served chez Dench to oohs
and aahs. You whip up until almost stiff whatever quantity you
like of cream, then add to it a similar quantity of natural yoghurt,
and then sprinkle the top fairly heavily with that sticky brown
muscovado sugar. Cover it with clingfilm and leave it in the
fridge for an hour or so. When you take it out the sugar will have
dissolved and you stir it through a bit to marble the mixture. It's
utterly delicious, and no one can ever guess what it is. I'm quite
sure it no longer features on the Dench table, as it has incalculable
amounts of calories and lethal levels of cholesterol. We're all on
diets now. But for a glorious period it was the star of many dinner

parties. Jude loves food, but for as long as I have known her she's been on some stringent diet or other, being deprived of the tastes she likes most. In the throes of one of these regimes during *Plough*, she told Niamh Cusack this particular diet required the eating of porridge every day for breakfast. She then said she had discovered that Marks & Spencer did the most delicious porridge she'd ever tasted, which you simply had to heat up and eat. She showed Niamh the package. Niamh pointed out the porridge was made with full cream. Jude didn't bat an eyelid. 'But it's porridge. That's the main thing.' Nowadays she seems to have cracked the diet thing, and looks very svelte. At a recent lunch together she had shrimps, a lobster, and two glasses of champagne. She's found the perfect diet at last.

Apart from being a terrific cook of the most comforting kind of English food – I can still taste her fish pie – Judi is an accomplished needlewoman. She frequently brings her tapestries to rehearsal, and during note sessions or when she's not on, her needle plunges briskly in and out of the material. I'm not sure whether the rate at which she stitches is an indicator of all going well or we're in trouble. Both, I expect, depending on the circumstances. She makes the most beautiful cushion covers. During *Plough* she gave me a present of a cushion tapestry kit, I think in the hope that it might be comforting. Patiently, she taught me cross-stitch, claiming the whole business was so simple you could do it in your sleep. A lot of years later, I still haven't finished it. I did all the easy bits around the border, but once I started the actual picture I got into a hopeless mess when a lot of different colours became involved. I have seen Jude stitch away at a very complex pattern, drop it as her cue came up, and walk onto the set and do a scene that would have us in tears on the sidelines.

Great as Jude's gift is, I would not like to imply that all those extraordinary performances were easy for her to create. During the rehearsals for *Plough*, for example, she hit a bad patch. She and Sam Mendes had a very good relationship. This was the second or third time they had worked together. Their relationship was playful but respectful, Sam's direction firm and robust. They were evenly matched. Most days were a satisfying mixture of hard work and fun. On one particular day Judi was unusually quiet but, when asked, denied that anything was the matter. During the afternoon, she suddenly burst into tears and said she didn't think she could do it. In another actor this might have freaked the rest of the company, particularly as we were nearing our first run-through, but we had no doubt she could do it. It was just a matter of finding her way. Judi has no sense of her own greatness, and makes no effort to protect it in any way. She has no problem allowing herself to be vulnerable in front of her fellows. This is one of the elements that makes her acting so truthful. In the event, Bessie Burgess' death was unforgettable. She crawled under a table to die, as if an animal seeking a cave. Again, when I came to play the part, I had to fight with myself not to do the same thing, so definitive was her performance.

In 1988 Ken Branagh and David Parfitt's Renaissance Company began rehearsal for three plays, *As You Like It*, *Hamlet* and *Much Ado About Nothing*, directed by Geraldine McEwan, Derek Jacobi and Judi Dench respectively. *Much Ado* was the first play to go into rehearsal, and I often sat on after my scenes had finished. I was still a Shakespeare novice, unsure of my grasp of The Rules, anxious to learn as much through observation as practice. Judi was adamant about the application of The Rules, a stickler for the metre. She would beat it out, softly, on the tabletop. During one of the scenes, one of the actors had picked up a rehearsal hat, a lady's straw, and put it on to help with some bit of business he was trying to work out. In time he became accustomed to it and forgot it was on his head. He came to a particularly serious scene, requiring a measure of gravitas. The scene seemed fine to me. I glanced across at Jude and she was helpless with silent laughter, tears pouring down her cheeks. It was the hat. To be honest, I can't remember much about those rehearsals apart from a great deal of falling about laughing, but that's mainly, I think, because I didn't have a very big part. The production was enchanting, and a huge success for her as a director.

During the course of the Renaissance season Judi was made a Dame of the British Empire. We decided as a company to make her an appropriate tiara, even though we were not quite sure whether this was mandatory headgear for a Dame. She has an enormous collection of bears, of all shapes and sizes, displayed in a deep windowsill in her house. Hearts, too, are a recurring theme, their shapes and images appearing frequently whether as objects in her home or as gifts to others. A combination of both seemed perfect tiara material. We collected as many hearts and bears of suitable size, as we possibly could and our designer converted them all into the most wonderful concoction. It looked like something from the hat rack of a very eccentric fairy queen. We presented it to her with all due ceremony while belting out, as loudly as possible, 'There is nothing like a dame'. She had brought her ribbon and medal, and asked Richard Clifford, who was playing the Duke, to wear it on-stage, which of course he did. I wonder if any member of the audience noticed. Someone once, years ago, had referred to her as Miss Drench by mistake. I sent her a multicoloured teapot. On one side it said 'Dame Judi Drench' and on the other it said 'Now Available for Panto'. As far as I know it still sits on her dresser.

When I first met Judi Dench, I was very much in awe of her. She became my model of the ideal woman and the ideal actor. She was the person I most wanted to be like. I had never lived in London before and was missing my home and family, particularly my son. Judi invited me into her home, included me in her own family life, wrapped me generously in their warmth. She was twelve years older than me, but a great deal older in experience, both in her career and in her life. I couldn't possibly think of her as an equal. I kept her on a pedestal for a long time, until I realised that with a real friend you have to stand on the same level ground, otherwise it's not friendship, it's a kind of dependency. Where before I was in awe of an icon, now I can be awed by her humanness, the depth and breadth of her talent and her heart. A long time ago, I felt the hairs on the back of my neck rise when I discovered that the word 'theatre' came from the Greek 'teatron', meaning 'to make visible the Divine'. This is what Jude does in her work, but it's also what she does in her life. She manifests love. She is incredibly generous with her self and her time. So many people and causes want a piece of her, and she tries to satisfy as many as possible. Perhaps being a Quaker gives her a certain responsibility to duty but, if so, it's duty propelled by a great love. And it may be that being a Quaker also gives her that most precious commodity, time to stop and be silent.

It is extremely difficult to write about Judi Dench without sinking into constant hyperbole, difficult to find anything to offer as a counterbalance. There is just one small thing. Visiting the Williams' house in the country without my car, Judi gave me a lift to the railway station. As we moved at a reasonable pace through the winding country lanes, I gradually began to realise that from time to time, rather often really, Jude didn't seem to notice the nearness of an approaching bend, say, or perhaps her position on the road, maybe quite far out from the kerb. There are some people who drive very fast with whom one feels perfectly safe, and others who drive at a moderate speed but induce sweating palms within seconds. Next time I had to go to the station, Michael drove me. On the way, unprompted, he said, 'My wife is a wonderful woman, and I love her dearly but, dear God, she's a terrible driver.' That was a long time ago, she's probably got the hang of it since then. But I was quite relieved recently to learn that now she has a driver.

One of Jude's greatest gifts to me, and perhaps to many women, is her modelling of how to grow old with dignity. Our business only seems to value youth, and in her negotiation of all those questions of to dye or not to dye, to lie or not to lie, to have just a little bit planed off here and there, those of us coming behind have a positive image of the possible. It seems to me that Jude is permanently in touch with the centre of who she is. Perhaps this place is her instinct, or perhaps it's her heart, or maybe they live in the same place. But coming from that place makes her straight and true. And if I can touch that place in myself, and remember to keep in touch with it, my hope is that I too can grow old with grace. Her talent is a gift of the Divine, her brow kissed by God, a rare benediction given to few and, as such, impossible to emulate or envy. One might as well be envious of a flower. But her heart, and the love that radiates from it, are her own, and she shares them with everyone.

Feeling What She Feels

HUGH WHITEMORE

*I*t was her energy that surprised me. You could feel it like summer heat through the soles of your shoes when you step off the plane at a Mediterranean airport. It was the first London preview (in 1983) of a play I'd written called *Pack of Lies*. Judi was playing an ordinary lower-middle-class housewife from a London suburb, and of course she portrayed the ordinariness with the greatest integrity, but what astonished me (and everyone else in the Lyric Theatre) was the formidable intensity she brought to the role. 'I've never seen such grief,' said the photographer Zöe Dominic. And, indeed, neither had I.

It is, I think, almost impossible to describe in words what makes a great actor great. By its very nature it's a quality that defies precise definition; something insubstantial, fleeting – magical, perhaps. But at the same time, something powerful and dominating and tough. I once asked John Gielgud who was the greatest actor he had ever seen; he thought for a few moments and said, 'Lucien Guitry.' His parents had taken him (aged about twelve) to see the great French actor, and he had never forgotten it. 'But why?' I asked. 'What made him so special?' Gielgud was momentarily at a loss for words. 'He seemed to grow,' he said, 'as I looked at him he seemed to grow – physically.'

At the time I found that a wonderfully evocative response; looking back, I can see that it actually *means* nothing; but it does convey something of the elusive quality that so impressed the teenage Gielgud. If I were asked to say what makes Judi so special, I think I'd reply: 'She seems to be acting only for me.' In other words, she's a great communicator. A very contemporary quality. (Somebody once said, and I think correctly, that David Frost's particular talent is the ability – knack? gift? – to talk to his audience as if there were no camera: direct communication, from him to the viewer with no impediment.)

Leading actors of past generations seemed to be rather distant and aloof, even such warm-hearted individuals as Sybil Thorndike or Wendy Hiller. One would admire their artistry, and be moved by it, but with Judi one seems to feel what she feels. This was particularly so with *Pack of Lies*, or at any rate, that is what her performance eventually achieved.

Pack of Lies began its life as a television play called *Act of Betrayal*. The BBC producer Cedric Messina introduced me to a young journalist (and later, gardening expert) called Gay Search. As a teenager in the late 1950s Gay had lived in Ruislip (a west London suburb), next door to some friendly Canadians called Helen and Peter Kroger. Gay and her parents became very fond of the Krogers – they soon became Gay's adopted 'Auntie Helen and Uncle Peter'. It was, therefore, a terrible and numbing shock when Mr and Mrs Search were told by the British Secret Service that they suspected the Krogers of being Soviet spies. (This was the height of the Cold War, remember; espionage was a deadly reality in those distant days.) Mr and Mrs Search were informed that MI5 intended to use their house as a place from which they could observe the Krogers and gather incriminating evidence. They were advised not to tell their daughter about these arrangements (they did not) and to maintain their friendship with the Krogers.

This must have been an appalling strain, particularly for Mrs Search, who saw Helen Kroger on a daily basis. The MI5 plan worked; the Krogers were arrested, imprisoned, sent back to Poland, and eventually exchanged for a British spy who had been arrested in Moscow. But these events had a lasting and grievous effect on Mrs Search; she died of a heart attack a few years later, still young, in her fifties.

The television play, which treated the story as a dramatised documentary, was a satisfying success, and that, I thought, was that. But then, about ten years later, Margaret Thatcher led this country into the Falklands War, a decision I passionately opposed. I remember walking around Camden Town Market on a Saturday afternoon. All the market-stallholders had switched on their portable radios, and were listening to Members of Parliament debating the war. (Yes, Parliament *was* called on a Saturday afternoon.) As the radio voices echoed around Camden Market, I reflected on the powerlessness of the ordinary individual. A government declares war and we can do nothing about it, no matter how wrong we may judge the action to be. That's democracy, we're told, we elect a government and they make the necessary decisions. But we didn't elect Mrs Thatcher to send the British navy sailing off across the Atlantic any more than we elected Mr Blair to bomb the citizens of Baghdad.

We have no real voice, I decided, not even someone like me who earns his living writing for the most influential medium of communication the world has ever known. I also thought of my mother, a woman of great courage and moral strength. Like so many people of her age (born 1906) and background (lower middle class) she had a natural and unshakeable respect for authority. Throughout her life, she did as she was told. But surely authority should earn this respect?

My mind flicked back to thoughts of Mrs Search and the bullying (albeit gentlemanly bullying) behaviour of MI5. I decided to rewrite *Act of Betrayal* for the stage and to develop this particular aspect of the story. We re-titled it *Pack of Lies* because Harold Pinter had recently written a play called *Betrayal.*

Here is a speech I wrote for Barbara, the main female character of the play. ('Bob' is her husband.)

Bob's mother was such a frail little lady. I never knew his father, he died long before we met. He was a clerk with an insurance company. She lived alone, Bob's mother, she lived in a small, draughty house in Maidstone. She came to see us twice a year, but always left after a week – 'I don't want to be any trouble,' she'd say. It was the most important thing in her whole life: not being any trouble. When her roof leaked, she refused to tell the landlord. 'He's been very good to me,' she said, 'and I don't want to make a fuss.' Even when she was ill and dying, she wouldn't ring the doctor after six o'clock in the evening. She'd just lie in bed, all alone in that miserable house, more worried about making a fuss than anything else. Her life was governed by fear, bless her heart. She was afraid of annoying the doctor, afraid of irritating the landlord, she was afraid of post office clerks, bus inspectors and anyone in uniform. And, like a child, she thought if she kept very still and didn't make a fuss, nobody would notice her. And she was right – they didn't.

Judi delivered that speech very simply. She just stood on the stage, motionless, talking to the audience, sharing her thoughts and emotions with them. The effect was intensely moving. But as we all know, simplicity is the very hardest thing to achieve. Any actor with a reasonable technique can bound onto the stage and dazzle the audience with vocal and physical fireworks. It takes real strength to do nothing – or *apparently* do nothing. It also takes courage and abundant self-confidence.

To digress for a moment: *Pack of Lies* was punctuated by a number of speeches which the actors delivered directly to the audience. One of them (spoken by Barbara Leigh-Hunt as Helen Kroger) described the electrocution of the American spy Ethel Rosenberg. During the Brighton try-out, Eddie Kulukundis, one of the producers, urged me to cut this speech. He felt it was so disturbing that it interfered with the narrative flow of the play. I disagreed and we had a fairly impassioned argument back-stage during the interval. Eddie is a good man and a good producer. He recognised that if I felt so strongly about the speech, then it should be left intact. He said so as the play ended, and asked (generously) if I would like a lift back to London. 'No, no,' I said gruffly and ungraciously, 'I'll make my own way back.' Little did I realise, as I sat waiting on a chilly platform for the last train to Victoria, that when Eddie said 'lift' he meant exactly that: he and his friends were winging their way to London in a helicopter.

Looking back, it seems inconceivable that anyone other than Judi could have played the leading role in *Pack of Lies*; indeed, Michael Redington, the producer, Clifford Williams, the director, and I all agreed that Judi would be ideal casting for Barbara, but, alas, she was playing Lady Bracknell at the National and wouldn't be available for about a year. So we submitted the play to some of the most distinguished actresses on the British stage, all of whom turned it down; but they took so long to reach their decisions that we realised Judi's year at the National was fast running out. We decided to try again. Judi's husband, Michael Williams, saw the script lying on his agent's desk – the agent he and Judi shared – he took it home, read it, and persuaded Judi that they should both do it, playing the husband-and-wife leading roles. (When the play opened and Judi received rapturous notices, one of the actresses who had turned it down sent me a postcard: 'Oh dear,' she wrote, 'what a mistake I made.')

We rehearsed in a working men's club in Chiswick. Judi worked quietly and diligently. I don't remember her asking for any changes in the text. The questions she asked were almost always technical. 'Should I walk upstage before she speaks? When should I switch off the light?' She seemed to slide into the character effortlessly. There was also, I sensed, a steely confidence that was both reassuring and slightly daunting. I was, I think, a little afraid of her. Whether or not she felt confident is really not the point; it was the sort of confidence that exists even when your knees might be knocking together with First Night fright. In her heart I'm sure she knew, or felt, or intuited that she had the guts and sensitivity and sheer bloody talent to deliver the goods.

Michael Williams virtually disappeared into the role of Bob. He gave a truly remarkable performance, reminding many of my colleagues of Ralph Richardson at his finest. The accomplished cast began to breathe life into the words I had written. Lord Snowdon came and photographed us. Ralph Koltai's set was being built. Props were being assembled. Clifford Williams sucked on his pipe and gently but firmly shaped the production, creating an impeccable verisimilitude of suburban daily life. Throughout the play Judi was called upon to make cups of tea, prepare vegetables for supper, do the washing-up. 'I've never done so much housework,' she said.

We all travelled to Brighton for the pre-London run. There was the poster outside the Theatre Royal with a sticker proclaiming 'Prior to the West End'. I walked gingerly into the stalls. There was the Koltai set. There were the actors in costume. The play existed. It's always an odd moment for a playwright. During rehearsals writer and actors are all together in the rehearsal room, sharing problems and jokes – a team. As soon as the production moves into a theatre, lines of demarcation are drawn up. The actors occupy the stage and the dressing rooms. The writer sits alone amidst the acres of empty stalls.

The early performances in Brighton didn't exactly fill me with optimism. On the first night an actor was so overwhelmed with nerves that he made his exit through the fireplace. At another performance, the lighting mechanism went wrong. Every time any of the characters switched *on* the light switch, all the lights went *off.* I shall always remember the look of helpless despair on Michael Williams' face as he stood on the stage, victim of electrical events far beyond his control. (Pre-West End performances are always a nightmare; I recall an ashen-faced Glenda Jackson sitting in her dressing room at the Richmond Theatre when she was appearing in my play, *Stevie.* She gave me a baleful glance and said, 'With any luck the theatre might burn down.')

Friends and associates drove down to see the play and we sat over supper while they delivered their (not always welcome) verdicts. 'Well, it's very good,' said someone close enough to me to tell me the truth, 'but I do hope Judi does something *more*.' But what could she do? I had written a play firmly based on reality – the reality of Ruislip and middle-class life, which, as we all know, is intrinsically un-dramatic. I lay in bed in my hotel room, head throbbing with too much red wine, and began to worry. Perhaps the play should have remained on television. Perhaps it's all my fault. Perhaps I haven't given her enough ammunition. I could imagine the reviews. ('It seems a waste of Miss Dench's great talent that she should be trapped in so drab a play.') I woke up sweating with anxiety – which was made worse when I realised that we had less than a week to go before the Press Night in London. But the die was well and truly cast. There was, I decided, nothing I could do.

'How do you feel?' I asked Judi as we all assembled at the Lyric Theatre for the dress rehearsal. 'Like Finty's hamster,' she said (Finty is Judi's daughter). Finty's *hamster*? Was that good? Was that bad? What did she mean?

The one really good thing about the Lyric Theatre in those days was the salt beef café in Windmill Street, just opposite the stage door. It was owned by a middle-aged man with sleek (dyed?) brilliantined black hair who must have been a professional boxer. I can think of no other profession that provides you with such flamboyant cauliflower ears.

'Working round here?' he asked, after my fifth or sixth visit.

'At the Lyric Theatre,' I replied.

'What's on there?'

'A new play with Judi Dench.'

'Ah – she's great,' said the retired boxer. 'What's the play like?'

'I wrote it,' I said. (What else could I say?) My host gave me a long look, but said nothing. I felt, with some alarm, that if the play failed he would hold me personally responsible.

The dress rehearsal was satisfactory. Ralph Koltai's set looked great; nobody made any major mistakes (no more exits through the fireplace); Michael Redington seemed relatively cheerful. I suppose I was expecting a modest success.

We had two previews before the Press Night. Up went the curtain and within a very few minutes it became heart-stoppingly clear that Judi was giving a great performance. Not just good – astonishing. Something extraordinary had happened. She had found a hitherto hidden power. Barbara, the Ruislip housewife, was still being portrayed with sympathetic integrity, but there was now an extra dimension to Judi's performance. It was as if she had intuitively understood all the various unwritten ideas and emotions that had gone into the writing of the play – which I have tried to describe in the preceding paragraphs. She embodied the courageous qualities of my mother (whom she had never met), she gave voice and presence to all the rages and resentments that I felt as I walked round Camden Market on the eve of the Falklands War (which I had never told her about).

It was also an extraordinary technical achievement. When the original play had been produced on television, I had employed a number of visual devices to sharpen the narrative. A significant close-up – a hand trembling on a door handle – a sudden cut to a facial reaction. Somehow, and I don't know how, Judi managed to achieve the equivalent of these televisual effects onstage. One was drawn, I suppose by sheer force of personality, to a detail of gesture or behaviour that gave the drama an extraordinary intimacy. The theatre with its Edwardian decorations seemed to disappear. One felt physically present in the semi-detached house where the story was taking place.

As that first preview came to an end I looked with delight and astonishment at the applauding audience. The warmth of their ovation was remarkable. I could see a well-known theatre director on the far side of the dress circle. He was on his feet, cheering. 'What has Judi done?' I whispered to Clifford Williams. 'Her performance seems entirely changed.'

'Whatever she's done,' said Clifford, 'we should all be bloody grateful.'

Of course her performance hadn't really changed; it had been sharpened by the presence of a West End audience. She was like an animal scenting prey. I've never asked her about it, but I suspect Judi was unaware of what she did. As with all real artists, it's the animal instincts that rise up and create those rare moments of greatness.

The Press Night came and went in the usual blur of anxiety and excitement and greeting people whose names you can't remember (or perhaps never knew). The reviews were unanimously excellent. The play was a success. Or was it . . . ? Success is something that's always recognised retrospectively. In actual fact *Pack of Lies* got off to a slow start. There were anxious meetings in Michael Redington's house with everyone wondering why the bookings weren't better. Then two things happened. *The Spectator* gave us the perfect one-liner for press advertisements: 'The West End at its best'; and the *Evening Standard* published the nominations for its annual Theatre Awards. *Pack of Lies* was nominated in almost every category. The box office phones began to ring, there were queues for returns, and large cheques arrived in my bank account every week. Judi played it for about six months and won every award available. She deserved them all and I shall always owe her the most enormous debt of gratitude.

A year or so later she gave another remarkable performance in the film we made of *84 Charing Cross Road*. Perhaps it was even more remarkable because (a) she wasn't the lead, and (b) the role was thinnish (to say the least). When she received the screenplay, she phoned the director David Jones and said: 'I'm halfway through – are you *sure* this is the right script?' Indeed, she had hardly anything to say, but her presence in the film was memorable. She played the wife of a Charing Cross Road bookseller called Frank Doel, played by Anthony Hopkins, and spent most of her screen-time preparing food or busying herself around their modest suburban flat (almost a reprise of the housework in *Pack of Lies*). I had invented a little scene in which Frank Doel's wife serves supper. Frank samples a mouthful of cottage pie and says approvingly: 'Very nice, very tasty.' An identical scene appeared much later in the film (demonstrating, I hoped, the unchanging pattern of life in the Doel household). Judi found the line 'Very nice, very tasty' irresistibly funny. She is a great giggler and Hopkins is wickedly fond of jokes. The fact that David Jones managed to get that moment on film says much for his persistence and patience as director.

84 Charing Cross Road, which was based on Helene Hanff's enchanting book, is an unusual film. It is constructed around a series of letters telling the story of a friendship between Frank Doel and a New York book-lover (wonderfully played by Anne Bancroft). Adapting this as a film required me to create situations and scenes over which these letters would be read. Obviously the easiest way to accomplish this technically would be to get the actors to record their letters and then to play them over a loud-speaker in the studio so they could react appropriately. But Judi didn't like that. She chose to learn the letters and then acted her letter scenes in silence, with the text 'playing' in her head. I believe Anthony Hopkins did the same. Later it occurred to me that that is what we all do – actors and writers alike: we listen to the voices in our heads.

It's impossible for me to write about Judi without mentioning two of her greatest performances that I admired not as a colleague, but as a member of the audience, or rather the viewing public. The first was in 1966 when she played Terry in John Hopkins' great television quartet, *Talking to a Stranger*. Poor, unhappy, sexy Terry – exactly the sort of girl I might have met at one of the West Hampstead Saturday-night bottle parties I went to as a young man. I know I would have fallen under her spell, would have been infuriated by her, infatuated with her, and that she would have filled my lustful thoughts day and night until I was finally and miserably rejected. Judi brought Terry to life with such vivid reality that I felt I'd actually met her (Terry, I mean, not Judi). Under Christopher Morahan's inspired direction she gave one of the greatest performances ever seen on television.

(I must also pay tribute to John Hopkins, the creator of so much memorable TV drama. When *Talking to a Stranger* was first shown, George Melly wrote: 'if Hopkins wrote for the theatre instead of the box, he would on the strength of this achievement rate as our greatest living dramatist.' I couldn't agree more. Now, alas, John Hopkins is dead; and because of the ephemeral nature of television, most of his work is forgotten. *Talking to a Stranger* is a masterpiece of writing, directing and acting.)

Some years later, Judi appeared in *Langrishe, Go Down*, a BBC television film directed by David Jones from Harold Pinter's dramatisation of the novel by Aidan Higgins. The story is about three impoverished Irish spinsters in the 1930s, who live on a decaying estate, imprisoned by loneliness and pent-up sexuality. Judi plays Imogen Langrishe, 'a free spirit trapped in a tightly laced-up personality' said the *New York Post*. Another critic wrote of 'her blunt features and intelligent eyes – at once aloof and vulnerable'. Imogen has a passionate affair with a German student (played by Jeremy Irons), a young man who is her intellectual and social and moral inferior. Recently interviewed about the film, David Jones said: 'Judi had never been out of work since drama school, but early on, she was told she didn't have the right kind of face for films.' The same thing happened to Peggy Ashcroft, who had to wait for *The Jewel in the Crown*. An American critic described Imogen Langrishe as a 'secret sensualist' and said 'it is a pleasure to watch Dame Judi give herself with such voluptuous relish to a character in full sexual bloom.'

'Aloof and vulnerable' – 'a free spirit trapped in a tightly laced-up personality' – 'secret sensualist': her best work is full of intriguing contradictions. One is always aware of conflicting emotions and feelings stirring just beneath the surface. Judi has the honesty and courage to let us see this. Even in Bob Larbey's popular and much-cherished television series *As Time Goes By* these contradictions are still apparent. Beneath what can only be described as a lovable 'exterior' there's often an implacable strength in her gaze, a toughness of manner and resolve that sets her apart from the so-called 'ordinary people' she is so often called upon to play.

I remember smiling to myself as I watched her in a James Bond film. As M – head of the Secret Service – she had been kidnapped by the villains and locked away in a dungeon some-where off the coast of Turkey (I think it was Turkey). Everyone was very distressed. M was in mortal danger! But one look at those Dench eyes glaring defiantly through the bars of her prison told you that it was not she but her captors who were in real danger. She has the eyes and spirit of a survivor. And that, I think, is the quality that makes her so special. Vulnerable, yes. Sensitive, of course. Courageous, most certainly. Sexy. Great fun too. But, above all, a tough and resilient fighter. She battles through life and wins. A survivor.

A final story about *Pack of Lies*. One evening a member of the audience was taken ill in the middle of Act Two. He was carried out of the stalls, having suffered a heart attack. A week or so later Judi received a letter from the unfortunate man's wife. She apologised for disturbing the play and said that her husband was making excellent progress and would almost certainly make a complete recovery. 'We were so enjoying the play,' she wrote, 'could you please tell us what happened in the end?'

Humility and Humanity

MARTIN JARVIS

One evening in 1957, just as I was finishing my homework, my father came home from the office with intriguing news. He said that Alan Cullen, a colleague of his in the insurance firm, had been taken to the theatre the previous night. It was a Shakespearean production and apparently there was a girl in it who had been rather wonderful. Judi someone. Cullen had been the guest of a man who knew one of the actors. The play was *Hamlet* and afterwards they had gone back-stage. Dad told me: 'It's a rather different world behind the scenes, by all accounts. Cullen says that the actors and actresses are in and out of each other's dressing rooms and that he actually caught a glimpse of Ophelia in her underwear.'

Two ambitions were born in me that day. One: to become an actor and participate in such back-stage saturnalia myself. Two: to see this production of *Hamlet*. A week later I was permitted to take the 68 bus from near our home in Croydon all the way to the Waterloo road. After a fifty-minute ride, I got off almost opposite the theatre. In the winter darkness a vertical lighted sign seemed to announce: 'POLYPHOTO'. It wasn't until I'd crossed the street and looked up again that I saw it actually proclaimed 'THE OLD VIC'.

I exchanged my two shillings pocket money for a gallery ticket and, along with more than a hundred others, climbed ten flights of stone steps and eventually perched up there on part of a long backless leather seat, high in the gods.

The lights went down.

> '*Who's there?*'
> '*Nay, answer me; stand, and unfold yourself...*'

Wow.

I was mesmerised by Shakespeare's thriller in all its aspects. John Neville's great and moody Dane; Coral Browne's creamy cleavage, onto which we elevated spotters drew a direct and salacious bead. And then – there she was – Judi Someone, fragile, tender, white-gowned as Ophelia. Her voice, so young, so clear, so direct:

> *My lord, I have remembrances of yours,*
> *That I have longed long to redeliver;*
> *I pray you now receive them.*

And when she distributed rue and rosemary for remembrance, barefoot, I too became mad for her. I've been mad about her ever since.

At her feet.

In the 1970s I finally met her. I was, in fact, her customer and gave her two pounds. The occasion was a charity gala at the Duke of York's Theatre at which she was a celebrity programme seller. I was a member of the audience. In the foyer I avoided purchasing from several other notables, neatly sidestepped Derek Nimmo and Donald Sinden and made straight for the small figure with an urchin haircut dressed in a flowing chocolate-coloured gown. I proffered money and was rewarded with a dazzling smile, almost, it seemed, of recognition, plus a souvenir programme. I stammered my thanks, mumbled how marvellous she was in *London Assurance*, got pretty well knocked sideways by a second radiant beam and reluctantly moved on.

I had to wait at least two more years before I encountered her in the flesh again. This time, having been making my way as an actor, I was invited to take part in a charity benefit in aid of Prince Charles' Viking dig in York. The show was performed in front of a well-heeled audience that included HRH himself. My role was King Canute; Judi, as I remember it, was a Danish fishwife. We had no scene together, but at least we were on the same bill, if not exactly in and out of each other's dressing rooms. Lined up afterwards on-stage for the royal handshakes, I felt for a fleeting moment on a temporary, if not equal, footing as the theatre manager introduced us to the Prince: 'Your Royal Highness, this is Judi Dench, and this is, er, Michael Jervis . . .'

But, rather as my cod Danish accent had proclaimed on stage that night in the character of Canute, 'Der zee, it's comink nearer und nearer . . .' so I felt that the time and tide were approaching when I might perhaps act a scene with her.

In the event I had a call, not from the RSC but from *Jackanory* at the BBC. Would I participate in some television programmes of excerpts from novels and poems suitable for children? The other actor was to be – aaah – Judi Dench.

'When do we start?' I was on board faster than you could say Richmal Crompton.

The casting was eccentric and imaginative. Judi played everything from Peggotty to all of Billy Bunter's form-mates. And of course she read some Shakespeare ravishingly. I performed passages from *David Copperfield* and Ogden Nash, we had lunch together, tea together. We talked about plays and literature and our families and laughed a great deal about the joys and absurdities of being an actor. Our friendship was cemented in the laughter engendered when, after we had shot one particular scene, the boss of *Jackanory* appeared on the studio floor with a worried frown on her departmental brow. Judi had just recorded a bucolic piece by Laurie Lee in what seemed to me a perfect Cotswolds accent.

'Oh dear,' the executive was saying, 'I'm afraid we'll have to re-record the last line. We couldn't possibly transmit it for children at five in the afternoon.'

Judi and I both consulted our scripts. It all seemed innocuous enough. 'Where's the problem?'

'That last bit, Judi, where you say "shouting through the letter-box . . ."'

'Yes?'

'Well you – ah – said: "*shitting* through the letter-box . . .".'

'Oh my God! Oh no, that was acting in character!'

Judi re-shot the offending line, sacrificing the authentic sound for (it has to be said) an only slightly more tactful enunciation, and now with an unmistakeably naughty chortle in her voice.

On a bright summer day in 1982, an apprehensive group of actors stood in the rehearsal room at the rear of the Lyttelton waiting for the artistic director of the National Theatre, Sir Peter Hall, to make his appearance. We were about to embark on the read-through of Peter's much-anticipated production of *The Importance of Being Earnest* which would open in seven weeks' time. Judi, in what was considered by some a daring piece of casting, was to play Lady Bracknell. I was Jack Worthing. I don't know which made me more nervous: the thought of working with Peter Hall, or the prospect of playing the famous hand-bag scene with Judi Dench. We all waited anxiously. Most of the space in the room was occupied by a strange sloping construction, rather like a motorcycle display team's take-off ramp. Thirty feet across and rising up towards the ceiling, its blue surface glittered in the artificial light. Probably something to do with the National's production of *Guys and Dolls*. This was going to get in the way unless they removed it before we began work.

Suddenly here was our director, entering the room beaming and nodding, a beneficent mandarin of the arts. I relaxed a little. I noticed Judi did, too. Peter has an enormous gift for making you feel the whole project is only possible because *you* are a participant. He greeted us individually: a kiss for Anna Massey, a hug for Zoë Wanamaker, both for Judi who stood a little apart, blushing slightly and grinning like a schoolgirl who might not have done her homework. Surprisingly, this was her first time at the National. The formidable Diana Boddington, stage manager and Lilian Baylis lookalike, herded us across to a long table down one side of the room.

We took our places and read the play through, stumbling a good deal over the text. Wilde's world was suddenly much harder to enter than any of us had imagined. We did our best. Nigel Havers' easy charm seemed just right for Algernon Moncrieff. Zoë read intensely as Gwendolen without looking up from the script. Anna, as Miss Prism, had clearly done a lot of preparation, her script decorated with coloured markings. Paul Rogers boomed authoritatively as Chasuble and Elizabeth Garvie sounded witty as Cecily Cardew. I found myself injecting Jack with a light-hearted airiness which I hadn't yet realised was wholly inappropriate. Judi read Lady Bracknell in a soft but spellbinding monotone which had people at the lower end of the table straining forward to hear. It was riveting. Her gift of total truth as an actress takes one's breath away. I knew, though, that until she has found the central core of a part she remains quiet and doesn't attempt a performance of any kind. She was very quiet today.

After we had finished, Peter told us he admired our efforts but the reading had been theatrical and artificial. 'Not Judi,' he added, grinning wickedly. He then talked about what he thought Wilde was trying to get at and what our approach should be. He believed that Wilde's plays reveal unattractive aspects of the underbelly of Victorian society; that the aphoristic banter is often his characters' attempts to mask the truths of their real lives. The epigrams are often a cover for something more sinister. They aren't just jokes. His point was simple and, in retrospect, obvious. It became clear, too, that a seriousness of purpose on the part of the characters actually increased the comedy of the play. *The Importance of Being Earnest* is 'A Trivial Comedy for Serious People', a drama of double existence, of hypocrisy and pretence, with buried truths lurking beneath the skin of each character.

Having completed his introductory chat, Peter turned to John

Bury, the designer, and invited him to show us the set. This is always the cue for everyone to gather round a small model and murmur appreciatively as tiny figures are moved about and bits of miniature scenery shifted to give an idea of what the real thing will look like. John rose, bulky and intimidating as any of the battlements he had created for countless Royal Shakespeare history plays. We expected him to bend down and produce his toy theatre from beneath the table. But no. He strode over to the foot of the glitzy motorcycle ramp. 'Here we are,' he said, blinking mildly behind slightly misty spectacles.

Judi and Anna gasped and looked at each other. Judi has always maintained since that day that it was I who voiced the thoughts of us all when I exclaimed, 'Is that it?' It was. This was no model. It *was* the real thing. Instead of appreciative comments and nods there was silence. If this incline were on the public highway there would surely be a roadside notice, 'Engage Low Gear Now.' We gazed. I knew we were all wondering how much acting could take place on a 1-in-5 gradient. And what on earth had it got to do with Oscar Wilde? I thought of a helmeted team of National Theatre dare-devils, led by Dench and Massey, their throbbing machines gathering speed, hitting the slope with perfect timing, soaring into the air across the tops of twenty-five London buses before landing on a similarly glittering escarpment at the other end. The Wilde Ones.

Judi and Anna were now beginning to look like two schoolgirls who were having real problems in harnessing their giggles. As we continued to stare, John Bury explained that in the first scene there would be a carpet on the slope, on top of which would be a small sofa and a couple of chairs. That would represent the 'luxuriously and artistically furnished' morning room of Algy's Mayfair flat. Nobody spoke.

'What about the garden scene?' asked Judi eventually, straight-faced.

John gestured up the blue hill.

'Just that?' bleated Nigel. John nodded.

'Yes, but the muffin-eating,' we cried.

'Oh, maybe a table.'

'On that slope?'

'Why not?'

'And chairs?'

John was getting tetchy: 'Well, we can work all that out.'

'John,' Judi enquired with vast politeness, 'may I ask why the slope is blue and glittery?'

He harumphed a bit and said something about the lighting he would be using for the garden. 'You know, that amazing depth of colour you get in the summer when the trees throw dark shadows across the grass.'

I caught Judi's eye. We all knew you can't play comedy if there isn't enough light. 'But grass isn't blue,' I managed.

Anna Massey leaned forward and whispered, 'They called him the Prince of Darkness at Stratford.'

A gurgle from Judi.

We began work next day. The unravelling of the text with Peter was infinitely fascinating, but life on the ramp was problematic. The rich accoutrements of Algy's rooms and Jack's country mansion were represented by a few sticks of furniture whose rear legs had to be sawn down to accommodate the rake. This allowed them to appear to be standing upright. The actors, incapable of being anti-raked in the same way, were forced to adopt awkward positions, knees bent, backs arched, trying to look natural. Walking was a challenge.

Judi, on her first arrival in Act One, seemed to appear over the horizon as if she'd hiked halfway up Everest. One felt she might not have made it at all had it not been for the umbrella she carried that seemed to do the duty of an alpenstock.

The abiding image of Lady Bracknell had been created by Edith Evans who played it in the theatre in the thirties, with Gielgud as Jack Worthing. But for most people, her performance was immortalised in the stylish film of the fifties, still shown regularly on television. Whenever *The Importance* is mentioned, anyone, it seems, can mimic the inflection of Dame Edith's unforgettable delivery of 'A hand-*baaaag*!!!???' Hers was a joyous choice, now thoroughly patented, though not necessarily Wilde's intention in the scene; he puts only a single question mark at the end of the sentence and no exclamation mark. But how to say the line with confidence any other way? Especially when the audience is waiting, eager to see and hear what another actress will do with it. If it's a carbon copy of Dame Edith it will seem merely imitative. If it's glossed over it will be a disappointment. During the early rehearsals, Judi muttered the line and moved hastily on.

After a few weeks, Peter decided that we should run the play for the first time. Judi, apprehensively it seemed, took her place at the top of the slope in readiness for her entrance. Nigel and I played the scene before she comes on, finding that the seriousness of purpose we had been working on was having some effect. But no one was quite prepared for the impact that Lady Bracknell was to have on us. Here suddenly was a neat, crisp, bird-like woman whose darting eyes took in the situation at a glance and whose sweet smile belied the power she wielded. This was a sexy, barely middle-aged mini-matriarch, who flirted outrageously with Algy, clearly her favourite nephew. Her voice was flute-like, her attitude to her daughter's future prettily pragmatic. A beguiling Bracknell that owed nothing to theatrical tradition yet seemed entirely the essence of Wilde's monstrous figure of controlling motherhood. Judi, before our eyes and ears, was redefining a character that had seemed impossible to shift from beneath the long shadow cast by Edith Evans.

Judi Dench's sensual Lady Bracknell was a triumph. Wearing a sharp little hat that still had room for a couple of dead birds on its brim, she continued to throw dazzling new light on the play and her character. Her invention was sublime. In the interrogation scene Lady B assiduously writes down Worthing's possible qualifications in her notebook. But when it becomes clear that a young man who has been born, or at any rate bred, in a hand-bag, has no chance of acquiring the hand of her daughter Gwendolyn, Judi tore up her notes and tossed them to the floor. A revelatory moment which the audience loved.

Even after we had been open for several weeks, Judi still confessed to being nervous of the audience's reaction to Lady B and of the dialogue that leads up to the hand-bag revelation. I thought she played it exquisitely, almost coquettishly, as Worthing seems more and more of a catch for her daughter. She took notes in the tiny book and, on hearing that I had been *found* – 'Found!' (she looked up with a serrated edge on that) in a hand-bag, she seemed not to believe what she was hearing. She repeated quietly, quickly, dead-pan, 'A hand-bag?' which increased the level of comedy and moved her on to the sardonic amazement of 'The line is immaterial.'

One night something strange occurred. We were playing the famous scene. As usual, I was planted halfway up the slope, legs and feet angled to accommodate the almost non-negotiable rake. Judi was seated centre-stage on the unsumptuous settee that tilted, on its anti-raked legs, towards the audience. Suddenly, before the historic line, and after I had announced, 'I was ... well, I was found,' I heard Judi exclaim: 'In what locality did this Mr James, or Thomas, Cardew come across this hand-bag ... ?'

Eh? It was as if we had suffered a small time-slip. My brain raced. We shouldn't have reached this point yet, I told myself. Had I inadvertently jumped half a page? Given the wrong cue? No, I didn't think so. Had she simply hurdled the line that always gave her so much anxiety? I wasn't sure. But whatever had happened, what should we do now? Go back half a page? Should I repeat the 'found' line so that we could swing into the hand-bag second time around? In the event we continued, both of us looking out from behind our characters with panicked eyes as the scene went on. Finally it ended and Judi made her exit. Nigel came on, eyebrow raised – they'd all been on tenterhooks backstage, wondering what happened – and we played the rest of the act. As I came off, Judi was still in the wings, waiting for me. She was almost in tears. 'Oh, Mart,' she said, 'what am I going to do?' I didn't know how to comfort her. I still wasn't sure it wasn't all my fault anyway. She went on, 'And what about the end of the play? It's all about the hand-bag and that you were found in it – and we haven't established it at all.'

I couldn't think what to say.

During the interval the six of us gathered in Judi's dressing room and spoke in low tones as if someone had died. Anna's face was the longest as she wondered, indeed we all wondered, how the end of the play would work. Lizzie Garvie opined that it wouldn't matter and she bet most of the audience hadn't noticed the absence of the hand-bag information anyway. They all know the plot. Privately I thought that Lizzie, though sweetly supportive, was wrong. Of course they'd all noticed. It's one of the most famous passages in English drama, and tonight it wasn't there. Without that section, the end of the play is meaningless. Diana Boddington's stentorian tones called beginners for Act Two and we continued the evening. By the time we reached the Act Three revelations, we were prepared for some puzzled reactions from out front. But, amazingly, the final section, the reference to Jack Worthing's bizarre beginnings, the story of the hand-bag itself and my fetching it from upstairs, went as well as it had ever gone. None of the laughs was missed and the evening ended on a note of relief from us and delight from the audience.

Afterwards we spoke to various people who had seen the performance. We were astounded to find that many had been unaware that anything was amiss, and that others had assumed those lines had been cut by Sir Peter. They all knew the play anyway, they told us. Canny Lizzie was right. But I know that, each night, Judi still dreaded that section of the scene and wasn't happy until she was striding off up the blue slope, flinging the dismissive 'Good morning, Mr Worthing!' over her shoulder.

She never failed to receive an exit round.

Michael Frayn's delicious play about a weekend in the life of a British sales team, *Make and Break*, was a major BBC television production in the middle eighties. The setting is a German hotel suite during a trade convention and centres on the representatives of a firm that markets 'demountable partitions'. Robert Hardy played the managing director. Judi Dench was Mrs Rogers, his secretary. I played Frank Prosser the publicity man. It's an extraordinarily perceptive comedy in which Frayn examines ways in which we attempt to impose our ideas on the world around us. A recurring image in the play is the team's precious module of a moveable and changeable set of doors mounted on a podium. They can be opened, closed, slid, swung and generally man-oeuvred or manipulated into a variety of configurations. A metaphor perhaps for an infinitely changing world.

As we gathered for the first read-through, Judi whispered to me that she hadn't actually read the whole play yet but that Michael (Williams, not Frayn) had said it was a marvellous piece of work and that she absolutely must do it. The reading was a hugely impressive event and I noticed many a tear being wiped away as we came to the final scene and the unexpected climax of the sales force's stay in Frankfurt. Such was Judi's truth as an actress/reader/interpreter that all the sad blessedness of Mrs Rogers' lonely life was fully encapsulated in what was, virtually, a sight-reading. There's a speech in the play when she is encouraged to talk about herself and her obsession with 'getting things done', whether it's office work, or preparing her meal at home in the evenings.

When I make myself supper in the evening I always cook myself a proper meal, and I always try to make sure I really enjoy it. I wouldn't enjoy it if I knew I'd still got all the washing up to do. So I wash up everything I can in the kitchen as I go along, and I put the meal on a tray, so I can just pop it back in the kitchen afterwards and wash the last bits and pieces up in the morning with the breakfast things. But the trouble is when I do sit down with the tray in my lap what I'm thinking is, Well, I've just got this little bit of eating to do and then I can put the tray back in the kitchen . . .

Judi's inhabitation of so many aspects of this lonely woman was remarkable. As we watched and listened to her during this impromptu first reading, there wasn't, I'm sure, one person in that room who wasn't both smiling at the warm absurdity of Mrs Rogers or crying at the way Judi somehow lived, heartbreakingly, deep inside the character. She was conveying something about the inner self of – was it Mrs R, or was it Judi D? Something infinitely moving, indefinable, yet wholly present. This of course is the mark of a truly great actress. Sometimes when I see her in the theatre, I find that I have a lump in my throat even as she makes her first entrance; then, seconds later, I'll be laughing as she throws out a line with impeccable, apparently spontaneous, truth-filled timing.

It is – or she is – a gift from God.

I worked with Judi most recently on a rainy April night in the West End. The occasion was the 2004 Centenary Gala in celebration of the life of John Gielgud. A number of actors who had worked closely with Sir John had willingly agreed to perform excerpts from plays or parts made famous by him. The evening was to raise money for the Royal Shakespeare Company and for RADA, both of which were dear to John's heart.

Judi had already been playing at the Gielgud Theatre for some months as the Countess in the RSC production of *All's Well That Ends Well*. Our one-off theatrical happening also included appearances and reminiscences from Sir Peter Hall, Sir David Hare and Alan Bennett. Paul Scofield performed Prospero's final speech from *The Tempest*, Rosemary Harris flew in from New York with a bagful of memories, Sir Ian McKellen became a Gielgudian Richard II. Barbara Leigh-Hunt and I recreated that joyously dangerous hand-bag scene from *The Importance*. Many of actor Clive Francis's superb Gielgud cartoons appeared in the handsome souvenir programme. The editor of this book, John Miller, devised the presentation, Joe Harmston directed and Ned Sherrin was the narrator.

However exciting this was, not only for us but for the packed house, all of whom undoubtedly loved and revered Sir John, my other abiding memory of the evening is of Judi herself. She provided, in the most unforced way, a gentle hospitality for us all. Her dressing room door remained open throughout the performance and, after each of us had done our celebratory onstage bit, we couldn't help but drift inexorably into her room, where she dispensed champagne and sparkling humour. At one point Peter Hall, Donald Sinden, Ian McKellen, Michael Pennington, Ronald Pickup, Barbara Leigh-Hunt, Barbara Jefford, Ian Richardson, myself, plus RADA students who were not only appearing in the gala but also acting as back-stage helpers, were all ensconced, quaffing merrily. We listened attentively from time to time to our colleagues on the tannoy, though a second, alternative gala continued among us, encouraged by our hostess, as further Gielgud stories (and countless tales of his legendary bricks) bounced from wall to wall.

Judi told of Sir John's generosity to her in the face of directorial intransigence when she acted with him in *The Cherry Orchard* more than forty years before. She also spoke of the present – her gratefulness to Peter Hall when she found herself losing confidence just before opening in the current *All's Well*. She related how she had rung Peter and, in tears, said she couldn't get a handle on the role and felt unable to play it, and how he had brilliantly talked her through the part and its problems so that, literally, a day later, things fell into place and her nerve returned. Amazing for us to hear this, having seen the production and witnessed one of her greatest, most sensitive performances. I was reminded of that same humility and humanity when she battled with similar feelings of inadequacy in trying to unlock the key to Lady Bracknell.

And now here she was: giggling, discussing the arts, the problems of funding, ticket prices, the importance of attracting young audiences, proudly telling of her daughter Finty's burgeoning career as an actress; then opening another bottle of champagne, remembering Johnny G, reminiscing about our time at the National together, the jokes and the close-knit camaraderie of the company. Actually there is never *not* great harmony present in any company headed by Judi.

She is the leader of our profession.

Earlier that same April evening, as I stood in the wings next to the prompt corner, I happened to look across the open stage towards the other side where I could see a small figure, waiting in the shadows to make an entrance. Hard to discern for a moment. Who could it be? Barefoot certainly. In a long white dress. Ophelia perhaps?

And then just as I'm thinking, of course, it must be one of the pretty young drama students, the demure creature darts onto the stage and into the light.

Judi.

Elfin.

Ageless.

Sexy.

Titania.

She begins to speak. Her voice, so young, so clear, so direct.

> *The spring, the summer,*
> *The chiding autumn, angry winter, change*
> *Their wonted liveries, and the mazed world,*
> *By their increase, now knows not which is which.*

I can't take my eyes off her.

I'm choked.

At her feet, again.

A section of this chapter, relating to *The Importance of Being Earnest*, has been adapted (though substantially rewritten) from Martin Jarvis's *Acting Strangely* (Methuen).

Circling Like a Plane

TIM PIGOTT-SMITH

$\mathcal{I}$ first began to love and admire Judi as an actress in *A Midsummer Night's Dream* at Stratford in 1962; she was a fabulous Titania, glamorous, funny, naughty, sexy. I can still hear her throaty gurgle as she lay with Bottom! That year we moved to live in Stratford-upon-Avon, and I was introduced to her in the High Street. I happened to be carrying the morning's newspaper and in it, by coincidence, there was a review, I think for *Measure for Measure*, in which Judi was playing Isabella. I mentioned that there was a nice notice for her. She stiffened and, resisting the impulse to grab the paper from under my arm, said, 'May I see it, please?' I gave it to her, she read it voraciously, looked relieved, thanked me and gave it back. She then spoke briefly of the production, of how brilliant her fellow performers were.

On another occasion, in the Green Room of the Royal Shakespeare Theatre, where I worked in the paint-shop one summer holiday between school and university, I met her again. Of course, I was so in awe of her that I could barely speak, but once she had met me, she always gave the impression of remembering me. Certainly, in spite of the great gap between us – I was a greenhorn, obsessed by theatre, and she a successful actress – she was one of those people that I felt I knew. Felt I always had known. I think this gift is central to her power as a performer. Quite apart from having a voice that you would die for, great eyes that communicate feeling and thought over distance, controlled emotions that are always readily available, astonishing and invisible technique, bubbling energy, breathtaking and accurate instincts, a great sense of humour, impeccable timing and a naughty sexuality, she is, underneath all these attributes, someone you feel you know.

I first worked with her in 1986. Although by then I had known her on and off for over twenty years, it was nevertheless a surprise to discover, as we mounted the stairs of the National Theatre for the read-through of *Antony and Cleopatra*, that I didn't know her at all. To my amazement, she was as nervous as a kitten. And of course, the ability to surprise is the final gift of the great performer.

During our hundred performances of *A & C* (I was playing Octavius Caesar), she won every major award going for her Cleopatra: a lot of people had thought her miscast – were *they* surprised! She was also made a Dame that year. The dressing rooms at the National are on four sides of a square, facing in on each other. It is one of the pleasantest features of working there that as you prepare for, say, *Antony and Cleopatra*, you can see, across the square, Alec McCowen making up for *Waiting for Godot*. On the evening that Judi's Damehood was announced, we all leaned out of our dressing room windows, and joined in a chorus of 'There is nothing like a Dame!' I did two plays with her at that time, so I was able, during our year together, to observe something of how she works, as well as discovering what a remarkable woman she is. First, the work.

We had an extended twelve-week rehearsal period for *A & C*, which was novel: it meant you could move slowly, and hold back decision-making till you felt secure. It was an unprecedented luxury, insisted on for this vast straggling play by Peter Hall who directed. This holding back is, I think, Judi's natural way of working – she manages to do it (it requires nerves of steel) even in an ordinary, four- to six-week rehearsal period. She circles, like a plane looking for the runway, waiting for some internal Traffic Control to give her the word to land. She knows she can deliver. She waits to discover some balance between what is possible and what is needed.

When she's exploring a scene, she plays it quite quietly, thoughtfully. Her mind and her instincts rove around. She will ask questions, some basic, some perceptive, and ruminate the answers. She does not make it difficult for other performers, she is fully there, she gives eye-contact, and plays the lines generously, but she seems to be holding back on decision-making. I think she is waiting for something inside to click. When she does decide, it is largely by instinct. She calculates the size of the plane; she senses the length of the runway, the speed of approach. She feels her way towards what the part, the play and the production require, and that decision, once made, takes hold of her. All this is sheer presumption on my part. I might be quite wrong about it, but that is how it seems to me from having watched her.

This theory of mine was to a degree confirmed for me by Hugh Whitemore when we were talking about Judi one evening. He said that throughout rehearsals and early previews of his play *Pack of Lies*, in which Judi performed with her husband, Michael Williams, it was Michael who was the star. He was a wonderful actor – Petruchio, Orlando, the Fool in *Lear*, Henry V: packed with charm, charisma and depth of feeling. Hugh said that Judi gradually grew in strength, and by the time the play opened, her 'plane' had landed, and she was giving a major, show-stealing performance. I can hear her denying this – 'Don't be utterly ridiculous!' It is vital that you understand clearly what I am saying: this is not a silly actress wanting to be better than the rest, motivated by ego and a desire for the limelight. I am not describing a calculating upstager who resorts to tricks to steal the show. This is just Judi, finding her performance, coming in to land. Rather than a plane, it might be more accurate to describe her as a bird of prey hovering around its potential victim, and then swooping in for the kill. It is what she does, and who she is, and it is as inexorable as a force of nature. It is her talent. It consumes. There is nothing anyone can do about it – not even Judi herself. It is her character. Her character . . .

The set for *A & C* contained a high tower, a monument, where Cleopatra takes refuge towards the end of the play. Caesar's soldiers besiege her there. Giving in to the inevitable, Cleo surrenders. In order to leave the tower, Judi had to be handed down some twenty feet from the main platform of the tower to the stage. That's a long way. And Judi is not tall. When we came to this moment in the technical rehearsal, I happened to be sitting with Judi in the stalls, watching proceedings. Peter had hired a stunt-girl to stand in for Cleo, to help choreograph this tricky moment with the fight director. Judi and I sat and watched for a good half an hour as they worked out how to get the stunt-girl Cleopatra – Judi – from the tower to the stage. It looked daunting. It looked terrifying. Frankly, it looked impossible. Judi and I just sat. Neither of us spoke.

They did it slowly, trying different ways, looking initially for whatever was feasible, and then for the least dangerous solution. One of the soldiers managed to get a footing halfway up the tower, acting as a bridge between the girls handing Cleo down, and the soldiers waiting to receive her on the ground. It no longer seemed impossible, but it still looked scary. When they were satisfied that they had worked out how to do it safely, they were ready to try it at speed. As the stunt-girl shot down, Judi grabbed my arm. 'Oh! Help!' she said, under her breath. I knew how she felt. I was glad it wasn't me who had a double up there! There are people I have worked with who would simply have said, 'I'm not doing that,' and left the theatre! Peter Hall is a wise man, and never wiser than in such delicate circumstances as this. He did not immediately turn to Judi, but calmly suggested they do it a couple more times, *before* doing it with her. Gradually her grip on my arm loosened. When it came to the inevitable and unavoidable moment, Peter turned to her with a challenging grin, and said, 'Shall we have a go?' Judi got up without a word, although she was pale with apprehension, walked down to the stage, climbed up into the tower, and did it. No fuss. Nothing. Great temperament. Great example to a company. It looked terrifying. It *was* terrifying. But it was the job, and that was it.

People often say that Judi never reads the plays she is sent. I don't know if I believe that. I do believe that she would often ask Michael to help her with decisions. This must be just one of the many ways in which she misses him. That said, I don't think either of them had read the other play I did with her at the same time as *A & C*. This was *Entertaining Strangers*, by David Edgar, also directed by Peter Hall. This wonderful play offered me the part of a lifetime as the Reverend Moule – pronounced Mole; 'Moole,' as he pointed out punctiliously in the first scene, 'is a mussel.' The woman's role is interesting but slightly under-written. I could never quite imagine Judi accepting this part if she or Michael had read the play thoroughly beforehand. It is really about the two people, Moule and Sarah, but on the page, it is the man's play. In performance, of course, Judi's skills more than balanced the evening. But again she did not arrive at her performance until quite late on. She held back, hovering, until she sensed that the best, the strongest scene she had was her last. Moule was praying at the grave of his son. He looked up, and through the falling snow saw Sarah Eldridge, his lifetime enemy. Her last words to Moule in this great scene are:

For we must remember, must we not, that like trees men have roots and trunks, which thrust up to the sky, but also branches which stretch out to other men, and touch them. [Pause] For only thus may we divine – from what strange soil, may green things grow.

Judi played the earlier scenes to their full, of course, but she supercharged this last one, doing more with it emotionally than I would have believed possible. I cannot even read it without tears coming to my eyes as I remember. It was a lesson: astonishing to watch. A privilege to act with.

Had she read the play? I really don't think so, but imagine this scenario: it is possible that when Peter asked her to play Cleopatra, he said, 'And there's a wonderful new play I want you to do alongside it. What do you think?' Judi, without drawing breath, without even asking the name of the play, or even her character, would have said, 'Of course, Peter. If you think I'm right for it. I'd love to.' And when she discovered that the part was not quite on a par with Cleo, she would not have breathed a word to anyone. She got on with the job, and did it brilliantly. That response would certainly be true to her character.

In addition to being a great actress, Judi is a normal person. This is a balance that is very difficult to achieve. And very rare. She is a real bonus in a company. She treats everyone the same. She is direct, open and fun. She gives generously of herself. When she is thinking, she withdraws into herself. It is as if a curtain has been drawn around her. She creates her own privacy, in public. On the rare occasions that she is like this, you don't go near her. You know she is preoccupied. But most of the time, she is just great fun.

One day when Peter was a few minutes late for rehearsal, she said to the company, 'Right, tomorrow morning you all have to wear something red. Anything. But you *have* to wear red. And we all have to be in early so we can see how long it is before Peter notices.' This is an imperial command. It is not issued as one, but woe betide the un-red! So, next day, we all had red on. I was wearing a red badge. One person had red shoes on. It's really silly. It's like a gang of kids getting together to play a trick on teacher, and it unites a company in the simplest way. We were all childishly pleased with ourselves for having remembered to wear red, and there was a tangible sense of apprehension as we waited for Peter to arrive. For the sake of historical accuracy, I should report that Peter walked in and said, 'Why are you all wearing red?' The fact that teacher burst our bubble so quickly is not the point; the fun had been had, and the company had been drawn closer together. But keeping the fun going can be hard over a long run. This is something that Judi understands. To say that she embraces the responsibility of it makes it sound pompous. She just does it.

Judi doesn't just play games in rehearsal, she carries them on into performance, although never, to my knowledge, to the detriment of the play. Some days she would organise 'Hunt the Opal Fruit'. She would secrete a sweet somewhere, and you would have to find it. Sometimes, in the course of a performance, word would go out – 'Find the Opal!'

During one section of *A & C*, she had a period of nearly half an hour marooned onstage, at the top of the tower out of sight of the audience, in the company of her handmaids, Charmian and Iras. They got into the habit of organising a picnic during this long and tricky period. It didn't happen until Judi was well established in the part; she did after all have to finish the play – Cleo has a marathon last scene. But the picnic became an institution.

'What's on the menu today, Jude?'

'Wouldn't you like to know?'

Or, 'What did you have today, Jude?'

'That's for us to know, and you to find out. Envy will get you nowhere. And you won't be getting an invitation.'

This picnic was something that Miranda Foster and Helen Fitzgerald used to love – having fun with a great actress, who is being just one of the girls, during a great play; having fun with a great actress, just before she goes on to *be* great. And Judi in that final scene was stunning. I had two entrances into that last scene which I made through the auditorium of the Olivier. Most nights I just stood at the back and watched her. Cleopatra's great dream speech was incredibly moving. Night after night. Perfect verse-speaking. Balanced with deep emotionality. New-minted every time.

It was in this final scene that one night the black glove made its first appearance. This glove has acquired something of a mythological status. So just for the record, here is how I remember it. In honour of Dame Peggy Ashcroft's eightieth birthday a huge celebration was organised at the Old Vic. Many of the cast of *The Jewel in the Crown* got together to perform a sketch. We decided that each of us should wear something that reminded the audience of *Jewel*. That was why we were there after all, because that was when we had worked with Peg. Eric Porter, as I recall, wore an eye-patch in honour of Count Bronowski. I wore one black glove, and did false-arm-acting in memory of Ronald Merrick. Judi was around back-stage making her own contribution to the evening and this black glove of mine gave her the giggles. She has a most infectious, rather dirty laugh. And for some reason this black glove of mine really set her off.

As Octavius Caesar, my costume included a pair of black gauntlets. I used not to wear them in the final scene, the only one I played with Judi, but after the giggles at the Old Vic, it was, I must confess, more than I could resist. I came on one night wearing *one* black gauntlet, and carrying the other rather ostentatiously to point it up. Judi swears blind she didn't notice, but I know she did. When we dressed her daughter Finty up in costume, and got her onstage in *Entertaining Strangers*, Judi again said she hadn't noticed. Nobody believed her! This blank denial is part of her sense of fun. It's almost a technique. It's provocative. It's flirtatious. It keeps whatever the joke is going. It makes you think if she didn't see that, what do I have to do to *get* her to see?

Well, if she didn't see the black glove *that* time, I thought, next time, she will! I decided to put it in the basket of 'asps'. There was no way she could miss that! The glove was placed at the bottom of the basket, with the asps writhing around on top of it. From the back, I watched like a hawk that night, as Judi took the lid off the basket. Well, she gasped. Her hand went up to her mouth. The audience, of course, thought she was reacting to the asps. Not that night. She saw the glove. But still she denied it.

After we had finished our stint at the National, Judi had a first night – *The Cherry Orchard* at the Aldwych – and I sent her a black glove for luck. She never acknowledged it, and flatly denied she had ever received it! 'I don't know *what* you're talking about!' she said to me on the phone. Oh, no? The night that my wife and I went to see the play, we were having a drink at the interval, and the Company Manager approached us to say hello. As he shook my hand, I realised he was holding something in his. He gripped my arm to make sure I didn't let go of it. 'Miss Dench sends her regards,' he said with a knowing smile. More than regards, she had returned the glove – the glove she denied ever having. And how clever of her. She did not know we were watching that evening. We hadn't told her we were coming. When she had found out we were in, she had connived with the Company Manager, at the same time as giving a wonderful performance as Madame Ranevskaya.

The glove has gone through many incarnations in the nearly twenty years of its life. Its greatest appearance, its apotheosis, you might say, was recounted by Kevin Spacey on the *Parkinson Show*. He was filming in Alaska with her. I sent him the glove. He went to no end of trouble, and 'gloved' Judi during a scene she had on a toilet! For the full account see *Parkinson*.

Let me tell you of one day in the life of the glove. In 1995, I was back at the National, playing the Earl of Leicester in Schiller's *Mary Stuart*. Judi was at the same time in the Olivier, sending in the clowns in *A Little Night Music*. We got to the end of our run, our last two performances of the Schiller, on a Saturday matinée and evening. The Sondheim company also had two shows that day, although they were remaining in the National repertoire for some time. At that time there was only one glove, and I had it. I did a lot of advanced planning.

For the matinée, I arranged with a chum to give Judi the glove onstage, during the performance. I knew it would come back to me that day. I knew that Judi would be aware that I was finishing, and would be determined not to remain in possession of the glove when our production ended, and I left the theatre. So it was no surprise that the servant who helped me off with my boots that afternoon, also forced something small, black and leathery into my hand, before bowing and running off. I had the glove back. So far, all was according to plan.

I had plotted with my friends Angie, Greavesy and Emma B on Olivier Stage Management, and in the evening performance of *LNM*, they made sure that when Judi unfolded her table napkin in the big dinner scene the glove would be there. Delicious. I fully expected to get the glove back again before our final curtain came down that night, but to my surprise, it did not arrive. This was not what I had expected. Funny, I thought. Unlike Judi to give up on our game – leaving me the winner! Their show finished, and she waved good-bye to me from her dressing room, and blew me a kiss as she left the theatre. No mention of glove. But the kiss was a bit much, and I thought she looked rather smug.

That night, the *Mary Stuart* cast had a leaving party, in the course of which Collin Johnson did a very witty cabaret. When he called me up onstage, I knew. Judi had of course slipped the glove to him. You had to hand it to her, sorry about that, she was on the ball! She had got it to me, after she had left the theatre. I couldn't give it back to her. Or so she thought . . .

From a metal coat-hanger, I had fashioned a wire frame in the shape of a hand. I eased this frame into the glove, got the Security boys to let me into Judi's dressing room, and planted it in her window-box. It was three days before she saw it, and when she did, I am reliably informed by her dresser that she screamed. It's not often you outsmart la Dench!

This game is increasingly hard to play – dreaming up new ways of 'gloving', and discovering new forms in which the glove can materialise. Michael Byrne gave it to her onstage in *Filumena*, Jamie Glover helped me get it to her in *All's Well*, up at Stratford. She threw it on the stage in front of me at a Gala in Regent's Park. She has sent it to me encased in perspex. She presented me with a black glove birthday cake. And one day a large box arrived at our home in the post. In it was a beautiful soup tureen – Pam and I were celebrating our twenty-fifth wedding anniversary – and Judi sent this generous gift; she is fantastically kind. When we took the lid off, there, inside, was an unsigned card with love and congratulations, and . . . the glove.

What staggers me about Judi is that she manages to fit this game into her crazy schedule. She is phenomenally busy professionally. She is also devoted to Finty and her grandson, yet she makes time for everyone. The truth is that I do not know Judi closely. I wouldn't call myself an intimate friend. I have known her for a long time. I adore her, but I am just one of many people lucky enough to have worked with her, with whom she stays in touch. Not one of us knows how she finds time for us all. We just marvel at her.

One day, when we were researching *Entertaining Strangers*, the National organised a coach trip down to Dorchester, so that we could see for ourselves the real places where our story unfolded. David Edgar's play is based on fact, and this research day was very helpful as we developed the feel of it. Judi was playing Sarah Eldridge, and the Eldridge–Pope brewery was most hospitable to us. On the way back, our coach pulled into a service station for a tea break. Afterwards, back on the coach, Judi was in stitches. We asked her what it was. Whilst buying a snack, a woman had walked up to Judi, stared hard at her and asked, 'Weren't you Judi Dench?' It's a gloriously silly question, to which there are many answers, not many of them printable. I can't remember what Judi said, if indeed she was capable of speech. She probably just laughed at her. She was killing herself on the coach.

If she did speak I'm sure she was polite, if a shade wry. She would certainly not have lost her cool. In fact, I have never seen her lose her temper. I have seen her go icy – when Parkinson went too near the bone, she turned to ice. That is what she does, she freezes. She exercises fantastic control. Some internal portcullis comes down. It is very dignified, and can be quite frightening.

Judi is also resourceful. You don't become and stay a leading actress without great inner strength, and behind all her fun, all her warmth, her thoughtfulness and unmatched generosity of purse and spirit, there is, I believe, a very strong woman, admirably strong. But so much of this is guesswork, because she is extremely private. The only time I have ever seen her crack was at Michael Bryant's funeral. It was not very long after her own Michael's death, and the event was too much for her. So she left. Very fast. Without any fuss. She kept it to herself.

When she was on Broadway doing *Amy's View,* and I was in a theatre literally across the road doing *The Iceman Cometh,* we used to meet for dinner occasionally. You might see a shadow pass over her face, or touch her voice, the shadow of her fear, concern and love for Michael, who was then so tragically ill. But that was a very rare glimpse inside, and always tempered with positivism. In addition to whatever else I feel about Judi, I have profound respect for her. On and off stage. I am just a little bit nervous that I might have gone too far writing about her now. I hope not. I would not upset her for the world. But the truth is, she is so private that it is quite *hard* to write about her. Hard to know what she really is. *Who* she really is. All that is left is conjecture!

Let us then continue to conjecture, and imagine what might she have said to the woman at the service station. Perhaps we should have a competition to find the best answer.

Question: 'Weren't you Judi Dench?'

Answer: 'Judi Dench? Who was she?'

Or perhaps: 'Who *is* she?'

Darling Judi.

Like No Other

NED SHERRIN

When an earlier generation of Dames was disappearing up into the great Green Room in the sky, I used to play a game of spotting their heirs. Maggie Smith echoed the high style and some of the commanding eccentricity of Dame Edith Evans, salted with Coral Browne's whiplash wit. Vanessa Redgrave had a lot of Dame Sybil Thorndike's force and political commitment. Eileen Atkins could have played Dame Flora Robson's roles, adding her own unique humour. Patricia Hodge conjured up glimpses of Gertrude Lawrence.

What theatrical ancestor to propose for Judi Dench? An easy parallel is Dame Peggy Ashcroft. Many of the lyrical roles are shared. The ever youthful voice is common to both. In both cases the greatness is unquestioned and the screen success came late; but somehow I always came back to that most loved and revered of popular Victorian and Edwardian actresses, Dame Ellen Terry.

The comparison is in public perceptions not in roles or in achievements. Judi never played, as Terry did, the boy Mamillius in *The Winter's Tale* for Charles Kean in 1856, or Puck or Prince Arthur in *King John*: nor has she doubled Good Fairy Goldenstar and Bad Fairy Dragonetta in the pantomime *The White Cat* or given her Cupid in *Endymion*. Ophelia became Terry's signature role with Irving. It came to Judi Dench too soon and she struggled at the Old Vic after her debut in the part.

Ellen Terry has Katharine in *Henry VIII* and Desdemona over

137

Judi Dench. Terry played Desdemona first with Irving, then with Edwin Booth, with Irving as Iago. Both men seemed more suited to the Ancient than the Moor. Ellen Terry played Katharina in a trial run of *The Shrew* with Irving; but it was Garrick's version, called *Catherine and Petruchio*. Judi has avoided both versions.

Dame Ellen Terry should have been a wonderful Viola but 'she acted wanly due to an infected thumb'; Irving's Malvolio was 'too painful to be funny'. The production ran for only a few nights at the Lyceum where the audience amazingly hissed the curtain-call on the first night. Dame Judi played Viola triumphantly all over the world, 'within a few minutes, long before her more famous moments, [making] it blessedly clear that she has the measure of the part'.

Terry never played Rosalind because Irving couldn't see a role for himself in *As You Like It* – Jacques too small, Touchstone too undignified. Dench, denied by inches, had to be content with Phebe – 'what an arse-paralysing part!' Both were triumphant Imogens, Irving staging *Cymbeline* in a rare moment of guilt over his partner's roles. The RSC production with Judi was not well received but her own performance was, 'blonde, impassioned and comely, Miss Dench is a divine Imogen.' The 'divine Imogen' was not best pleased when her director had to go immediately to America and was not around to tinker. To pick one word now from Michael Billington's review, she became 'impassioned' about it.

Ellen Terry had two goes at Beatrice. For both actresses there is the relevant cliché to drag out of the text: 'there was a star danced, and under that was I born.' Terry enjoyed her first outing in Leeds with Charles Wardell, who was to be one of her husbands. It was different at the Lyceum. 'I was not the same Beatrice at all. A great actor can do nothing badly, and there was very much to admire in Irving's Benedick. But he gave me little help. Beatrice must be swift, swift, swift! Owing to Henry's rather finicking, deliberate method as Benedick I could never put the right pace into my part.' Donald Sinden was more accommodating for Judi. He had consulted John Gielgud: 'Benedick is a very boorish fellow, you'll be much better than I was.' The critics shared J.C. Trewin's opinion. 'This is high comedy and no Beatrice in memory has been more firmly based in truth.'

Both actresses were successful Portias in *The Merchant*, though Irving clipped Terry's wings again. 'Portia in the trial scene should be very quiet. I saw an extraordinary effect in this quietness. But as Henry's Shylock was quiet, I had to give it up. His heroic saint was splendid but it wasn't good for Portia.' Although praised, Judi gave the play short shrift, she was 'Trevved' into it by the persuasive Trevor Nunn. 'It is the only play of Shakespeare's I dislike. Everyone behaves so badly. I wouldn't cross the road to see it.' She was directed by Terry Hands and disagreed passionately with Emrys James' interpretation of Shylock. This produced the epic note from the director: 'You mustn't be unkind to Emrys. His father was a miner.'

There are other shared roles. Hermione is one. Ellen Terry had to wait for Beerbohm Tree in 1906 when she was fifty-three for *The Winter's Tale*. Judi Dench was thirty-five when she doubled Hermione and Perdita, which only Mary Anderson had done before (156 years earlier in 1887). The reaction to Judi's performance? 'A presence which touches greatness.' Irving braved Romeo when he was forty-three, Terry's Juliet ten years younger. The production was a huge success financially but neither actor was happy with the performance. For Judi Dench Juliet, opposite John Stride in Franco Zeffirelli's production, put an early seal on her greatness. Ken Tynan's review and the audience response triumphed over earlier critical cavils. It also prompted a favourite Dench anecdote. One night when Juliet turned to Peggy Mount as the Nurse and asked, 'Where is my father and my mother, Nurse?' her real father stood up in the stalls and said reassuringly, 'Here we are, darling. Row H.'

There remain Volumnia and Lady Macbeth. Ellen's Queen was immortalised by John Singer Sargent; Judi's by a television film recording. Terry played in the long shadow of Mrs Siddons whose Lady was a virago. According to Nina Auerbach, 'The highly strung, tacitly feminine Lady Macbeth [Terry] played in 1888 was to be her richest, most searing commentary on herself in the role of womanly actress ... but she lost heart when her performance failed to communicate all she meant it to ... Lady Macbeth needs no unsexing to make her wicked: in her poise, her murderousness, her rage for power, and her untiring usefulness to Macbeth, she is "all over a woman" ... she coaches herself to tempt Macbeth in the same words with which the actress must often have walked onto the Lyceum stage, "be damn'd charming".' However, in an opulent Lyceum production she failed to convince her most sympathetic critics, Clement Scott in London and William Winter in New York. Only her father, Ben Terry, approved: 'My joy was prodigious. Always your loving Daddy.'

Trevor Nunn's Stratford production of 1976 was a revelation. Michael Billington summed it up: 'McKellen and Judi Dench as his Lady, in fact, usher us into a hair-raising, unmistakable presence of great acting and both are at their finest in the banquet scene ... it is one of the few occasions in the theatre when I have felt that combination of pity and terror one is supposed to feel in tragedy: these are not monsters but recognisable human beings willing themselves to evil and disintegration in the process.' Judi would have agreed with Ellen's reaction to the Siddons virago: 'I'm always against those Lady Macbeths who are so strong and evil at the beginning. If they can do it on their own, why do they invoke the spirits to help them?'

How Ellen Terry would have welcomed the intimate space of The Other Place and the Donmar. Her great-nephew, John Gielgud, prompted Coral Browne's crack when he told her that Judi Dench was to play Lady Macbeth. 'Oh,' said Coral, 'then I suppose we shall have "the postcard scene".' However, in his letters to Irene Worth, Sir John is fascinated by the prospect of the little actress in the small space: 'Ian McKellen and Judi Dench have the most extraordinary praise for their *Macbeth*, which

Trevor Nunn has brought to the Donmar. I should really like to see it – a "chamber" production without scenery or any kind of costume presentation, which is the way Peter Hall talks of doing Lear for me – perhaps.' Alas, he never did, but Judi and Ian McKellen struck vivid sparks.

The final shared Shakespearean role is Volumnia in *Coriolanus*, Irving's last Shakespeare venture at the Lyceum. Ellen Terry's Volumnia was not well received and while Judi Dench, playing with Kenneth Branagh, was praised, she was not able to mine for such delights as she was to discover later as the Countess of Rossillion in *All's Well That Ends Well*.

It is only necessary to list a few of Dame Judi's other roles to blow a hole in my comparison with Dame Ellen. The similarity is in public acclaim, affection and identification. Consider Judi's other range. She has played nearly thirty Shakespearean women, as well as directing three of the plays: *Much Ado* for Kenneth Branagh's Renaissance Company, *Romeo and Juliet* in the Regent's Park Theatre, and *Macbeth* for the Central School of Speech and Drama.

I was interviewing her one Saturday for the radio programme *Loose Ends*. Graham Norton, who was just setting out on a talk show career on the programme, was seated next to her. He had confessed to me beforehand that he had been a student at Central when she directed the Scottish play. His role was Ross. He wondered if she would remember him. We hatched a plot. I asked her if she had enjoyed the new adventure of directing. She had, enormously. We talked around the problems of the play and her solutions. Then I said, 'Who played Ross in your production?' 'Oh,' she said, 'isn't that usually cut?' You rarely see the Dame with even the smallest piece of egg on her face but she seemed to enjoy the experience. Collapse of distinguished party.

Irving found two farces for Ellen Terry, Réjane's famous role in Sardou's *Madame Sans-Gêne*, a lively washerwoman who becomes, under Napoleon, a lively Duchess; and *Nance Oldfield* which he bought for her. Yet William Archer wrote: 'this most charming of all our actresses of comedy has been translated into a sphere in which she is far from home.'

Terry was pithy about Irving who played Napoleon in front of tall furniture to make himself look small. 'It seems to me,' she wrote, 'as if I were watching Napoleon trying to imitate H.I. and I find myself immensely interested and amused in the watching.' Irving had been a dazzling comedian in his early days but at the Lyceum he associated laughter with ridicule. Laurence Irving, his grandson, admitted that 'in jilting the comic muse he was guilty of a grave breach of promise.' In limiting his co-star's access to great comic roles he made her suffer too. By staging *Madame Sans-Gêne* instead of Shaw's *Man of Destiny* he denied her the Strange Lady. Her only Shavian role was to be Lady Cecily Waynflete in *Captain Brassbound's Conversion*. After resisting it for years she played it in 1905 but liked the part no more than she had Barrie's *Alice Sit-By-The-Fire*, another role tailored for her.

Judi, on the other hand, has been happier in Shaw. Her St Joan in Nottingham in 1966, according to *The Times*, 'gave to Shaw's relentless but superbly innocent saint a touching and unusual quality of a charming child'. In 1975, in the rarely successful *Too True to be Good*, she played Sweetie Simpkins, the Cockney nurse who masquerades as a French countess. She brought an enchanting passion to the part. As Ian McKellen said: 'Shaw wants fully rounded acting, and he doesn't always get it, but Judi embodied this person and brought her totally to life, not as someone with a lot of bright things to say, but someone with a passion, and once you bring passion to Shaw he's revealed as a great playwright – he doesn't get the performances he deserves, I think.' Five years before she had coasted successfully through *Major Barbara*, spurred on by Brewster Mason's powerful Undershaft.

The easiest way to illustrate the range of her repertoire in comparison with Ellen Terry's is a random, not comprehensive list:

Kate in *She Stoops to Conquer*, Anya and Ranevskaya in *The Cherry Orchard*, Arkadina in *The Seagull*, Dorcas Bellboys in *A Penny for a Song*, Irina in *The Three Sisters*, Dol Common in *The Alchemist*, Amanda in *Private Lives*, Margery Pinchwife in *The Country Wife*, Lika in *The Promise*, Sally Bowles in *Cabaret*, Bianca in *Women Beware Women*, Grace Harkaway in *London Assurance*, Millamant in *The Way of the World*, Juno Boyle in *Juno and the Paycock*, Cecily and Lady Bracknell in *The Importance of Being Earnest*, Deborah in *A Kind of Alaska*, Mother Courage, Carrie Pooter in *Mr and Mrs Nobody*, Bessie Burgess in *The Plough and the Stars*, Desirée Armfeldt in *A Little Night Music*, Mrs Rafi in *The Sea*, Helen Damson in *The Gift of the Gorgon*, Christine Foskett in *Absolute Hell*, Esmé in *Amy's View.*

Judi had two other paths to popularity denied to Ellen. Alongside innumerable one-off plays on television she staked an early claim to small-screen greatness in John Hopkins' *Talking to a Stranger.* Then two enchanting comedy series sealed the home audience's love affair with her: *A Fine Romance* with Michael Williams and *As Time Goes By* with Geoffrey Palmer. Only the international, and particularly the American, audience remained to be conquered. The two Queens – Victoria and Elizabeth – collaborated in her triumph, aided by her elevation to M in the James Bond series and Iris Murdoch in *Iris.*

Somehow the Terry magic communicated itself to the British public by radiating out of the Lyceum and Irving's tours. The Dench magic has had the benefit of modern media distribution. Both by their different means became, in that stultifying phrase, National Treasures.

The only time that I worked with Judi and Michael was when I directed them in Keith Waterhouse's fine comedy, *Mr and Mrs Nobody. Mr and Mrs Nobody* is based on the Grossmiths' *The Diary of a Nobody*, the classic account of the genteel pretensions of lower-middle-class Victorian life recorded in the diary of Charles Pooter, and Keith's reply, *Mrs Pooter's Diary.* This began dramatic life as a Radio 4 *Woman's Hour* serial read by Judi. This was lucky. The Dame can rarely be persuaded to read a script before she starts to rehearse it. She preferred to rely on the judgment of Michael, or directors like Peter Hall or Trevor Nunn whom she trusts. She swears she had never read *Antony and Cleopatra* before putting herself in Hall's hands.

On this occasion, having been paid by the BBC for her pains she confided to the *Radio Times* that she would love to play Carrie Pooter onstage. Keith took this as an invitation to start adapting, using the spine of events described by Mr Pooter and constantly puncturing his self-regard with his wife's scornful asides. Michael Redington, who had recently produced Michael and Judi impeccably in *Pack of Lies*, accepted it with open arms. Michael and Judi persuaded the trusted Trevor Nunn to direct, but with his multitude of commitments he kept putting them off. When Keith's patience was exhausted he sent me a copy and we met at the Garrick to discuss it. I couldn't have been more enthusiastic, or more available, not having *any* productions in prospect, let alone Trevor Nunn's umpteen.

The play's single flaw was that it was greatly over-length. In researching his original Keith had amused himself poring over old bound volumes of *Exchange and Mart* and inventing contemporary household necessities for the Pooters like Neave's Varnish Stain Remover, *Jepson's Sunday Newspaper*, and an indispensable magazine, *Lady Cartmell's Vade Mecum for the Bijou Household*. The Pooters' favourite champagne was bought from 'Jackson Frères, importers of Fine Wines and Vintner's Sun-drymen. Runner-up, Isle of Man Bottlers' Exposition Medal 1883, Lower Ground Floor, Paxley's Varnish Warehouse, 235–239 Female Penitentiary Road, N., to which all complaints should be addressed.'

To Keith and to me 'Jackson Frères' soon became a synonym for cutting the text. In Keith's flat or mine we would settle down at about 11 a.m. with a bottle of champagne and savage the play. When we could cut no more we would leave it for a day and convene the next morning with another bottle of Bollinger/

Jackson Frères. We found that with fresh minds fresh swathes of dialogue could be culled. I remember *Mr and Mrs Nobody* as about a five-bottle job.

There was another snag. Although Judi and Michael shared Keith's impatience to get on with the play, Judi had a major reservation. Early in her career she had been much wounded by my old collaborator Caryl Brahms' reviews of her first performances. Caryl had identified, and perhaps over-emphasised, a school-girlish-jolly-hockeysticks quality in the young actress. She persisted in referring to Judi as Dench J. This rankled over the years and, although Caryl had died three years before, Judi was suspicious that I might have inherited her prejudice. Ironically one of the last performances Caryl saw was Judi's in Harold Pinter's *A Kind of Alaska* at the National. She phoned me on getting home late that night to say that she thought it was perhaps the greatest piece of acting she had ever seen by a woman. Judi's reservations did not reveal themselves to me at this stage or I might have been less keen to plunge in. However, there were other insecurities.

Mr and Mrs Nobody is essentially a two-hander but I added a silent maid, and a factotum to ease the mechanics of staging and a string trio in a minstrel gallery to create the atmosphere of a Victorian soirée. Judi loves a company and hates a quiet, empty back-stage. This gave her five more colleagues with whom to socialise.

She was still professing doubt as to whether she and Michael could hold an audience alone for a whole evening. One thing which helped to persuade them was Julia Trevelyan Oman's revolutionary idea for the set. At a preliminary reading (the time it took demanded another two-bottle cutting session of Jackson Frères) Michael and Judi were enchanted by Julia's scheme for a revolving set. She wanted the audience to see in turn all four of the walls on which her impeccably decorated treasure chest of Victoriana was to hang. It seemed so simple and so fresh a device that it won the day. All reservations were swept away. Sadly, we failed to find any machinery which could realise these unique theatrical effects and on the first day of rehearsal I had to confess to the cast that the revolve had been abandoned and we were left with a beautiful but static set. Fortunately it was now too late for the stars to pull out so they stayed to shine.

Working with Judi and Michael was a joy and a liberal education. Their different approaches were fascinating. Michael had to din the lines into his memory by endless repetition. He spent hours doing his homework while Judi effortlessly absorbed her part by a sort of osmosis. Once, after a timed run-through, we found that another Jackson Frères session was necessary. When the cuts were given she took her script and gleefully tore out the pages making the maximum ripping noise. A wince of sudden bereavement crossed Keith's face. Michael, having worked so hard to master the lines, was also reluctant to see them consigned to the waste bin.

Different approaches to preparation did not produce a different intensity. *Mr and Mrs Nobody* is both a tour-de-force and a tightrope walk for the duettists. The Pooters have to people the stage with imaginary neighbours, friends, City colleagues, tradesmen and their wayward son, Lupin. Michael and Judi agonised over exactly where the people they were addressing or describing would be, magically conjuring life out of empty spaces. It was an attention to detail which gave a rock-solid reality to the fanciful convention.

In contrast to her iron concentration in performance, Judi likes to talk about any and everything else until the moment that she steps onto the stage. Her favourite game, a sort of twenty questions played with the company manager, is to guess what 'names' are in the audience that night. This is stretched out if possible to a second before she makes her entrance.

At a charity evening at the Old Vic to celebrate Dame Peggy Ashcroft's eightieth birthday, I watched Judi stand by a pillar in the stalls enjoying the actors onstage throughout the first half. She was appearing in the second. I was surprised to see that she returned to her post after the interval and there she stood until Eric Porter, the actor preceding her, began his soliloquy. Only then did she slip through the pass-door, arriving upstage with just time to enter and rip off one of Dame Peggy's famous speeches.

Of course every actor has his or her own method of preparing before a performance. If Judi's seemed to be like jumping off a precipice and expecting to fly, that belies the intense work which she did during painstaking rehearsals. However, her openness in her very social, chatty dressing room ill-prepared Keith for a later Mr Pooter. When he called in to wish him luck, 'merde' or 'break a leg' before his opening night in a provincial theatre he was greeted by a frosty actor. 'Don't you realise they've called the half? How would you like to be interrupted in the middle of writing a sentence?'

The only time I saw Judi less than completely in control was for an instant on the first night in London when Michael leaped in to cover the moment of hesitation. As he said proudly afterwards, 'If Jude goes I turn to steel.'

It was a joyous experience. The Garrick Theatre was full for the run and the two stars were irreplaceable. Two bonuses for Judi were her heavy Victorian costumes and her energetic time onstage. She lost pounds during the run – splendid preparation for her Cleopatra which followed at the National, continents and centuries away from Carrie Pooter, but an even greater triumph.

In spite of Judi's heart-warming, heartbreaking voice, her virtuoso verse speaking, her power and her impeccable comic timing, two purely physical moments remain most deeply etched in my mind: her total, quiet, physical collapse when she realises the fate of her friends revealed as spies in *Pack of Lies*; and the moment at the end of *All's Well That Ends Well* when two hands move out a tiny way in involuntary welcome to Helena. It caught my breath on both occasions when I saw the play – and it had the same effect on my two companions.

I see I have paid scant attention to her glorious Cleopatra. Caryl Brahms and S.J. Simon must have been thinking of her forty-six years earlier when they wrote the last chapter of *No Bed for Bacon* which has a plot echoed in the film *Shakespeare in Love*. Shakespeare is offering to write a great part for his boy player whom he has just discovered is a girl.

> *'I am going to write a play for you.'*
> *Viola's spirits soared. 'Loves Labours Won?' she enquired.*
> *'No, no,' said Shakespeare quickly. 'Some other play – a play that needs a woman and cannot be acted by some prancing boy.'*
> *Viola tasted the idea. 'Will it be sad?'*
> *'It will be tragical,' said Shakespeare. 'It will be about the most fascinating woman who ever lived. It will be about Cleopatra.'*

Type-casting.

Life Forces

LAURENCE GUITTARD

When John Miller first spoke to me about making a contribution to this book honouring Dame Judi Dench, he suggested that I think of it as a sort of birthday card. I have followed that advice, and so what follows is mainly for Jude. I kept a diary for most of the year I spent working with her at the National Theatre in *A Little Night Music* and my hope is to awaken some happy memories of that extraordinary time.

My diary entries, as originally written, are quite terse. I have avoided the temptation to expand and explain them here, in order that the highlights of the whole run can be recalled. It is a mosaic which offers a glimpse into our company over the year that we played together.

'Played' is absolutely the correct word to use about the experience of working with Jude. In spite of many trials and one great tragedy, we 'played' when we were on the stage. It was fun and light-hearted and true, and so we were free to grow and be expressive in ways that sometimes took us by surprise. It is an ideal way to work, and one that I know is always at the heart of anything she does.

For most of you, who do not share these memories, my hope is that you will find some interest in a glimpse into our lives and work at the time. We were a team. Acting on the stage is a team sport, and Jude was the captain of the *Little Night Music* players.

Theatre-goers may be interested to note how often the quality of the audience is appraised in these dairies. It may surprise you to learn that just as you judge us when you come to see our work, you are also reviewed by the performers on the stage every time you sit down in a theatre. The audience is the life blood of our profession, no two are the same, and the ultimate quality of each night's performance has as much to do with who is watching, and what they bring to the event, as it does with the actors on the stage.

3/8/95 Time for some catch-up. There has been a frenzy of activity in my formerly quiet life. I have had an interview, and sung for Sean Mathias who will be directing a production of *A Little Night Music* at the National Theatre in London. I was hesitant about doing *Night Music* again as I had intended to leave that show in the past. It was a complete and fairly happy memory, and I felt done with it. The chance to play Fredrik not Carl Magnus, and a chance to work with Judi Dench made me ultimately decide to go in to meet Sean.

Some time passed without word and I figured that it hadn't worked out. Then suddenly I had the job, and almost immediately left for London which I found to be roasting in a blistering un-air-conditioned summer heat wave. The first week of rehearsals, some of which are being filmed by the *South Bank Show*, was spent looking for a place to live and trying to get settled. I now find myself living in Primrose Hill, which I think I will enjoy, and into my second week of rehearsal at the National. The cast includes Judi Dench as Desirée, Siân Phillips as Madame Armfeldt, Patricia Hodge as Charlotte, Lambert Wilson as Carl Magnus, Brendan O'Hea as Henrik, Joanna Riding as Anne and Issy Van Randwyck as Petra.

Today was a typical rehearsal day for Sean. We began at 10.45 with a company warm-up, first vocally with Mark Dorall, the assistant music director, and later dance with Wayne McGregor, the choreographer. Wayne is one of the most open and likable people on the production and embodies a genuine warmth and generosity that helps all of us to be less self-conscious and uptight about our dancing skills. This is followed by Sean's theatre games for one third of the company each day on a rotating basis, and usually a music rehearsal for the rest of the company, then lunch which is taken at the canteen within the complex.

It was my morning for music, and so I worked with Lambert on 'The woman was perfection'. It is very odd to be singing Fredrik rather than Carl Magnus this time, especially in the patter section. Many short-circuited entrances.

After lunch we completed the first read-through of the play. This has been unusual enough to suggest some comment. The entire company, including actors, designers, stage managers, choreographer etc., lounge on pillows arranged in a large circle on carpets which have been dragged into the room for the purpose. Each person in turn reads a line of the play, moving around the circle until the scene is finished. There then follows a lengthy discussion of what we have read, with anyone with (or without) a thought about the text putting in their oar. If there is a song, the lyric is divided and spoken in the same alternating manner as the spoken dialogue. Mark then plays (and, boy, can he play!) the music for the company, then the song is attempted either by the actor who is playing the role, or by everyone in concert if the appropriate performer is not prepared.

The read-through of this particular little piece has taken eight days.

7/8   After the usual morning shenanigans and a spot of waltzing we had our first real rehearsal. The first Egerman household scene. Joanna Riding, Brendan O'Hea and I were the first to walk the plank. Brendan, who should be a wonderful Henrik, has been asked to actually learn to play the cello for his number. This is madness! In spite of an unbelievably heroic effort (he has, amazingly, learned to play the notes of the solo part) it is an impossible task, and the Jack Bennyish result not exactly on the mark. Surely they should rethink this.

Although the slow relaxed approach has been extolled, there

is a lot of pressure and everyone in the Egerman household has been pushing like mad from the very first attempt. I found it difficult to lay back at all. This wreaks havoc on my usual approach, and has made me feel even more uncomfortable and feeble than hitherto. Hopefully, I can speak to Sean tomorrow, and get his help to come at this a little less forcefully. I wonder when I'll work with Judi?

11/8 Although the heat wave has returned full force, the week ended wonderfully. A fine first working day, with Dame Judi even more generous, easygoing and gifted than I could have imagined. We worked the scene in the touring digs for the first time, and it was a fine beginning. Judi has all the quirkiness and vulnerability that Glynis [Johns] brought to the role, added to a real specificity and a calm, centred, self-assured rehearsal technique. For the first time I feel at home and competent. May the fates continue to smile on us.

16/8 The rest of the day was spent interminably staging the top of Act Two. Everybody is involved, there is a great deal of coming in and out of focus and I'm afraid that the out of focus Desirée and Fredrik were rather badly behaved throughout the afternoon. We were constantly shushed and glared at by the powers, but unrepentant continued to whisper and giggle our way through a long, long day.

Tomorrow night after rehearsal, we're all going to watch the Bergman film which will be followed by a 'Swedish Evening'. It will feature Swedish food, drink and a handful of imported Swedish guests. Judi said that after a quick hello, presumably to the Swedes, she planned to vanish as quickly as humanly possible. Me too.

17/8 Another long day, culminating in 'Smiles of a summer night' and the dreaded Swedish Evening. Judi fortified a group of us in her dressing room beforehand with a bottle or so of champagne, and we ventured down to rehearsal room 2 for the festivities. First we watched the wonderful Bergman film, and then mingled with some rather (who can blame them?) self-conscious Swedes. The costume sketches were on display for the first time and look beautiful, and helpful. And so, following in the footsteps of the leading lady, with Abba ringing in my ears, I beat a hasty retreat.

17/8 Apparently, after Judi and I left the party last night the festivities, fuelled by a notable consumption of Swedish drink, reached riotous proportions, culminating in Paul shaving Sean's head. When our director finally appeared this morning, he wore a series of hats and wigs stacked on his head princess and the pea style. Finally, as the morning wore on, they were all doffed, and Paul's skilful tonsorial work shone bright in the fluorescent light of rehearsal room 2.

Hangovers faded and we got a good deal done as we worked through to the end of 'Send in the clowns'. Judi is really going to be wonderful in this part. It's such a lesson to work with her. She has this laser concentration, but whereas in most actors that kind of concentration seals them off, with Judi it opens her. Many discoveries become possible. So we work together and off each other, as it should be and rarely ever is.

23/8 Met Patricia Routledge after rehearsal for a quick bite, and then to see Judi in Rodney Ackland's brilliant play *Absolute Hell* (originally *The Pink Room* – better title). What a great night in the theatre. A production that could never exist under the prevailing conditions in the USA. Judi was sensational, and held the centre of the kaleidoscopic structure with ease and power. She was wonderful, as was Greg Hicks (an actor new to me) in the other central part. The enormous company was excellent top to bottom and played with generosity and a beautiful ensemble spirit. The play itself was a revelation; tough and funny, compassionate and just.

24/8   Long day at work. The *South Bank Show* was filming all day for Jude's tribute. We worked the Digs scene all morning with them looking over our shoulders. Not much work accomplished under the circumstances, but we had fun and lots of laughs. In the afternoon on our own again we worked the Carl Magnus section of the Digs. Lambert makes an excellent rather lyrical Carl Magnus, and I think it will be really funny.

We concluded the day with a run-through of the first act up to 'Liaisons'. It went surprisingly well.

31/8   While the orchestra rehearsal was in progress Judi and I were called away to work the 'Send in the clowns' scene for *South Bank* people. They have really been very discreet and unintrusive, but it is hard to rehearse when cameras are rolling. There is so much to accomplish in these short scenes, but I think we are finding the way. We both prefer to work without talking about it. We just go on and do it slightly differently each repetition. Just playing it as it happens, and it begins to find its own way. The process is one of the great mysteries of what we do.

11/9   Our final run-through in rehearsal room 2. Rather laid back and suffering from the day off. Nothing alarming, but none of us is particularly secure in the text, that's for sure. It is frightening to think that at this point in rehearsal, we have yet to achieve a single satisfactory run-through of the show. At least there is nothing to fall apart in the technical.

17/9   Just a few lines to catch up with myself. A week of endless twelve-hour technical rehearsals. The set by Stephen Brimson-Lewis is sensational and very beautiful. It has been designed to take advantage of all of the technical tricks the stage of the Olivier is capable of. There is a huge revolving stage, the core of which is divided into two elevators. One element can sink into the ground while another rises from below to replace it. It means that we will never be able to repeat the production in another venue, as this machinery is unique to this theatre.

We were due to have a dress rehearsal last night, but it was cancelled and the tech continues to grind on. Everyone is exhausted, but we are all in pretty good spirits. We desperately need a non-stop run-through.

18/9 The great day has come and gone. We were called at 12.15 to work for an hour or so, mostly on the set. Lunch, a short break, and then on to our first and only dress rehearsal.

I peered out front before we started and there was Sondheim, as rumoured, settled into the centre section stage right. The first we have seen of him. What we all most hope, of course, is that he will be pleased.

Dinner break, followed by our first preview. The audience was very affectionate and generous, and the whole evening went as well as we could have hoped, never having got through all of it before. When we took our hastily arranged call I saw Steve out front applauding like mad. My God, I thought, it looks like he really enjoyed it. I wonder if we will ever hear. We left the stage to return to the dressing rooms, but had to be called back for another bow. Maybe we've got a winner.

20/9 Another night of improved security (half as much sweat) and minor glitches. In the opening waltz the traveller failed to open, and as the dance music began we all were trapped behind a massive velour wall. When finally released, we somehow caught up with the music, more or less found the dance steps, and by a miracle finished almost confidently. In the Digs Jude and Lambert became attached to one another. His medals caught in her wig and so they played the scene more intimately than we had rehearsed it. In the second act 'Clowns' scene I started to lose my moustache, and so played the scene looking unaccountably upward and praying that it would not flutter impotently to the ground before I could get off. Jude, not to be trusted at moments like this, all but laughed out loud. Finally I was able to escape to the glue pot.

21/9 Tonight was the Royal Gala performance. A benefit at £250 a seat, with the usual frozen audience. By a miracle, and several hundred bottles of champagne at the interval, they warmed considerably for the second act and things finished pretty well. Hard first act, lots of enthusiasm at the end.

Although it was the last thing I felt like doing I struggled into my all-purpose grey double-breasted and scurried down to the celebratory dinner. There, to my delight, I learned that my name was not on the list for the dinner. I thought I would have a quick drink and beat it.

No sooner had I grabbed a glass of Sancerre than Jude arrived to discover, unbelievably, that her name was not on the list either. The list-keeper was unmoveable. I knew how exhausted we all were and thought she must be as relieved as I was to play hooky. She got a drink as well, and we stood on the balcony overlooking the lobby, outside the dining room, and had our first long talk away from work. Suddenly from the dining room a very determined Patricia Routledge appeared. She was not going to take this lying down, and within minutes she had dealt with the list-keeper, rearranged her startled table, and ushered us into the festivities. Later, as I was leaving, Routledge gave me a note on my performance. 'A little more hubris, I think, my dear,' she whispered as I left for home.

25/9 We rehearsed from 1.00 until 5.15, had a break, and then to the first performance of the week. The first act was going really well until 'You must meet my wife', during which Jude accidentally stepped inside the lining of her kimono. The result was that her shoulders suddenly jack-knifed towards her knees. She found herself trapped in a sort of hunchbacked crouch, and unable to walk except in tiny shuffling steps. I'm afraid we both lost it, and lost it so badly that the only way we could finish the number was by not looking at each other. We may never be able to look at each other again.

26/9 Opening night! We were called at three and did a warm-up with Wayne, and then with Mark. Then we formed our familiar circle, and Sean spoke some inspirational words. After a few theatre games (much to Jude's delight), we were released to eat and get ready for the performance which was earlier than usual, at seven o'clock.

Back-stage, the theatre was awash with countless flowers and gifts. My wonderful dresser/psychotherapist Tom said he had never seen anything like it. Everyone was ready to finally do this, and we gave them a good show. The audience cheered at the end.

Down to Jude's dressing room where many friends assembled and the champagne flowed. I met Jude's husband Michael Williams for the first time, and he was so generous and warm that I felt I had known him for years. I also met Paul Rogers, whose work I have always admired.

We all trooped down to the Olivier bar for further warm-up before leaving for the party which went far into the night.

3/10 As usual I did not read the notices at all, but it seems we are a big success. Rumours are flying. At the moment the most reliable is that we will extend through July. Jude said they asked if she would stay until then, and she answered that she would stay 'til a year July.

The performance took a while hitting its stride, but we gave a good show, I think, before a 'prove it' sort of audience.

31/10 Hallowe'en. Jude has given me an un-birthday present to be opened today. It is a handsome goblet. Etched round the rim are letters that read, 'STUBBORN, SLOTHFUL AND DIFFICULT TO PLEASE'. This came first from my joking (if too often accurate) description of myself to Jude in rehearsal one day (S and S), and my mother's comment about me in Jude's dressing room the night she saw the show (D to P). I can't remember when I was so pleased by a gift.

18/11   After the between-shows nap the real fun began. The second performance played before the audience from Hell! The late arrival of a large theatre party disrupted the opening scenes, and the slow dull blankness at the front dragged us down, down, down in the most distressing way. Not only did we have a great black hole out front, we also had a series of disasters onstage. In the opening cadenza Stephen Hanley lost the high note preparatory to totally losing his voice later in the act. At the top of the Digs a thunderous bang sounded (Jude suggested an assassin at the front) as a lamp overhead exploded. No one was injured. When I came off for my change during 'Liaisons' I was told that Stephen wouldn't complete the performance (couldn't complete) and that Joe, hastily changing costume, would finish the show. Simultaneously, Claire's voice deserted her, and my beautiful daughter Fredrika was suddenly a light baritone.

8/12   We had a brilliant cake for Jude's coming (9 December) birthday. It was the second act bed of roses, with Desirée on her back, black-stockinged legs 'in aria'.

17/12   In the early evening a group of us from the company went to the BBC to see the taping of the final instalment of Jude's TV series with Geoffrey Palmer, *As Time Goes By*. This was the conclusion of the series, which has been going for five years, so there was sadness in the air as well as affectionate high spirits. She was wonderful, as always, so easy and unruffled. It's a pleasure to watch her work the simplest material. Geoffrey Palmer is no slouch either.

18/12   Splendid show, before a splendid audience, the best we have had for some weeks. I really enjoyed myself. Especially the

Digs, and later, the bedroom with Jude. I'll just pause and be grateful for the good fortune that has brought me to this theatre, and given me the opportunity of working with this extraordinary woman. I feel like Bert Lahr. 'Where will I ever find another?'

30/12 Awoke feeling like death. Two shows to deal with, the last of the year. I dragged myself to the theatre, nausea, hot flashes and chills, aching muscles, the works. Got through the matinée. I thought that my mad dash up the steps from the basement for the quick change into the theatre scene would be my last act. I slept the whole time between shows. Somehow I got through the evening with Jude's help. She actually made the evening memorable by unveiling a 'Happy New Year' banner stitched round her middle when she opened her kimono for 'the page that has been written on'.

10/2/96 Difficult day. Jude came to the theatre in terrible pain. There is something wrong with her eyes. My guess is some sort of corneal abrasion. She was painfully photosensitive, and had to work more or less blind as she couldn't wear her lenses. She did a heroic performance, and went on to rest between shows.

Just before the second performance, a bomb went off at Canary Wharf. The explosion which could be heard in the theatre occurred at about seven o'clock. We were soon told that it was the work of the IRA, and that the tenuous truce which has held for seventeen months is ended. The performance was deeply affected by the tragedy. Jude was on painkillers for the second show and that seemed to help. Stephen Hanley was feeling terrible all evening, and was out for the last waltz.

12/2 Jude has a scratched cornea and, although she does seem better, is still in some distress. As Jude is unable to work with her lenses, Emma has taken to calling her Blind Pugh. Stephen was out with bronchitis so Joe was on. The audience was a difficult one, at least I thought so, and the performance felt strange. The revolve was behaving oddly at the top of the show. There was shuddering, and strange booming noises echoed from the depths. In the second act before the Clowns scene it failed to turn, so Tim acted as bed mover, and Blind Pugh was led on. Apparently the operator was asleep, as we later discovered, and so the final turntable cues were as they should be. Or more or less as they should be, as once a move is missed, all computer settings become useless. Two tomorrow.

(Starting on 4 March we went back into rehearsal to put in some new cast members who were to replace the actors who wouldn't be staying on for the extension of the run.)

4/3 First day back to school with the new kids. Sean spoke to us most sensitively and helpfully about the performance he watched last Wednesday. We did an hour's warm-up with Wayne's assistant, an hour of the dreaded games, and then settled in for some work on the Digs and the breakfast scene.

Jude had a cake brought in to welcome Sean back, and the new actors to the company. It features pillows round the rim, a bundle of sticks in the centre, and an inscription saying 'No more fucking bamboo sticks', or words to that effect.

It was announced that Stephen Hanley would be leaving us with the other departing cast members as a result of failing health. He has been working while suffering from AIDS, and doing a heroic job of it.

5/3 Second day of rehearsal with the new people. We worked the Digs with Simon who progresses rapidly. He'll be very different from Lambert, but hopefully just as funny.

Jude and I had a couple of hours off at lunch-time, and escaped. We went to the mezzanine for a proper meal and a glass of champagne. Then we hustled next door to the Hayward Gallery for a show entitled 'Spellbound'. In spite of much praise in the press it proved pretty silly, but we had a really good time of it.

Back to rehearsal for a disastrous dance session. There was nobody present who knows the staging of the musical numbers. As Wayne will not be here until the last day, we are in considerable disarray. Between us we can piece things together, but it is very time-consuming, and unfair to the new people.

18/3 A long and difficult day. We worked with Wayne from eleven until five and then did our last performance with the original company complete. Jude arrived this morning in slightly rocky shape. She's had an allergic reaction to a skin moisturiser, and is sporting a mouse bite on her finger.

We did a really fine performance with our departing friends. Sean made a surprise appearance as a servant in the dinner scene, and Jude's Mike was there for the second time.

We had champagne after, and another beautiful cake (this company is cake mad), and a chance to say good-bye. Tomorrow dress rehearsal, and opening with our new cast members. It will be a long day.

19/3 As predicted. An exhausting day but a more or less successful one. The new crew did well and most of the screw-ups came from the original people. I went hilariously up in my duet with Simon. I was so concentrating on him that I inadvertently jumped to the Carl Magnus words in the patter section of the duet. When I tried to jump back to mine, every lyric deserted me, and I continued in Esperanto to the end.

In the Digs, when we were rushing around at Carl Magnus' entrance, Jude suddenly vanished. I had no idea what happened until I saw her determined little form clambering up from the floor behind the bed. Both feet had slipped on the carpet and flown out from under her. The carpet muffled the sound of the splat as she hit the floor. I heard nothing. It also cushioned the fall so she seemed none the worse for it. But we were both destroyed. This falling over thing has happened before in 'You must meet my wife'. I turned to deliver a line to her and she was gone. It was another silent splat. Again she rose beaming from the floor and we both laughed out loud. It was a clever cover.

31/3 We had a company meeting about the cast album. Steve, who is in New York, says he wants it to go forward, but his lawyers have put impossible conditions in the way. As we still have heard nothing, we pretty much unanimously decided to decline the recording at this time. If they want to do it later, we can reconsider it then. It is a great disappointment.

6/4 Double header, and not bad. After the performance I went with Jude to her home in Surrey. A beautiful and peaceful place. The central part of the house and the barn were built in the seventeenth century. We had champagne with Michael and Finty and four excellent cats. To bed about three.

7/4 A Wonderful Easter Sunday. I awoke to bird song, and looked out my bedroom window to see a pond (invisible last night) with ducks and two swans in full sail. After coffee and a wash up, I went with Michael to the local pub for a warm-up, and a chance to meet some neighbours. All this is a world completely apart from the hectic, demanding life she leads, and surely is part of what makes it possible without total mental meltdown.

Mike toured me around the property and showed the work they had done and what was planned. Then back to the house where a delicious lunch was waiting. Does the world know that this woman cooks too? After a quiet evening I took the express train from Gatwick, and was back to the city in no time.

23/4 Back to work, and an event-filled evening. We did a sitzprobe at three o'clock. Jude is back from Barbados looking tanned and really rested. We did our various warm-ups and started at 7.15 as usual. When we reached the end of the prologue, the lift in the centre of the drum refused to do its stuff, and Ernie made an announcement to the audience that there would be a fifteen-minute break while they attempted to repair it. The Egerman family and Petra were fished out of the drink, and we all waited while fifteen minutes became twenty, and then twenty-five, all the actors nursing that perennial unfulfilled fantasy, a cancelled performance. Sure enough the elevator was finally fixed and we continued.

The audience, thrilled at participating in a disaster, was very warm and clubby. Things continued perking along until late in Act Two when Jude suffered a crushing spasm in her back and was in tremendous pain. She managed to carry on, and we finished with a seriously crippled waltz at the end of the show. This waltz, which is usually such a fun time for us, was more like torture tonight, but of course we must have looked funny and her groans occasionally turned to laughter as we finally reached the end. As we changed after the performance there was an ominous announcement that Jude's understudy Di Botcher should come to rehearsal at eleven in the morning.

I went down to see her after I got changed, and she seemed a little better. Finty was there. She had come to the theatre on a premonition that something was amiss, and was able to see Jude home.

27/5 My God, more than a month without an entry, and I left Jude, compromised, in a paralytic back spasm. Have no fear, she recovered and did in fact play the next day and all subsequent performances.

The big news is that we finally recorded the show. It was done last week, with performances following in the evening, so it was an exhausting workout for us all. There are always so many difficulties to overcome in getting a show recorded. The current practice of sealing everybody off in soundproof compartments so that the engineers can get a discrete track is very counter-productive for the performers. Jude and I had to record the whole last scene without being able to feel each other's presence, or even to look at each other, so I pray it's not totally dead in the water.

Trisha was in the grip of a horrible flu, seriously under the weather. She managed a pretty extraordinary job of it, but there was no way she could do total justice to her brilliant Charlotte. Siân Phillips was inexplicably required to do 'Liaisons' to a prerecorded track. None-the-less she still managed her beautiful rhythmic subtlety in the song. She is really ideal in this part.

Stephen Hanley came back to record his part. Seriously ill and quite weak, he sang magnificently.

7/7 Another long gap in the record. I keep a diary only on the road. Now, I really feel I live here, so I'm afraid it has been slipping away.

The company did a cabaret in benefit of AIDS charities on 24 June. I didn't sing, but rather played an ugly American heckler interrupting Jude and Brendan as they performed 'Sixteen going on seventeen' in Austrian costume. It was memorable! Unforgettable! The whole evening was a great success with everyone shining brightly.

Jude arranged a junket to Glyndebourne on Saturday. We started with lunch at her home in Surrey, and a delicious Fortnum & Mason's picnic between the acts of the opera which was *Cosi*. Black tie was required and being tuxless in England, I tarted up my black suit, and managed to escape detection. It was a charming production (shipboard) by Trevor Nunn. Musically it was up and down. Solveig Kringleborn, a Norwegian soprano who sang Fiordiligi, was the best.

We did our first eight-performance week. The end is in sight. We work four days starting tomorrow, and then the final push. Six weeks of eight performances each. It is hard to believe that my adventure is almost ended. Time is moving very rapidly. A little lifetime with a great acceleration as the end approaches. I shall miss this theatre and my new friends more than I can say.

Desirée in *A Little Night Music*: backstage with Laurence Guittard (Fredrik). National Theatre, 1995.

'Acting on the stage is a team sport, and Jude was the captain of the Little Night Music *players.'*

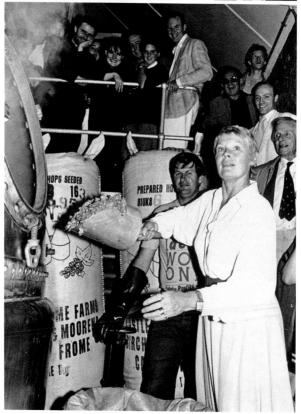

Researching *Entertaining Strangers*, with Tim Pigott-Smith and the company. National Theatre, 1987.

'Judi was playing Sarah Eldridge, and the Eldridge-Pope brewery was most hospitable to us.'

Filumena, with Michael Pennington as Domenico. Piccadilly, 1998.

'An hilarious mockery of Neapolitan machismo.'

Making-up for Esmé in *Amy's View*. National Theatre, 1999.
Photographed the night before flying to Hollywood for her first
Academy Award Nomination for *Mrs Brown*.

With Billy Connolly, who played John Brown to
her Queen Victoria in *Mrs Brown*.

*'You appear to be an immense agricultural Scottish person
whose Queen's shoulder nestles neatly under his oxter.'*

Winning the Academy Award for *Shakespeare in Love*, 1999.

'I feel for only eight minutes on the screen I should only get a little bit of him.'

*I*ris Murdoch in *Iris*, with Jim Broadbent
as John Bayley. Miramax Films, 2001

*'*Iris *was a film about enduring love. It wouldn't and couldn't
have been made without Judi as an actor and as a person.'*

The Countess Rossillion in *All's Well That Ends Well*.
Royal Shakespeare Company, 2003.

*'To listen to her deliver the text was to hear
a master class in Shakespeare's verse.'*

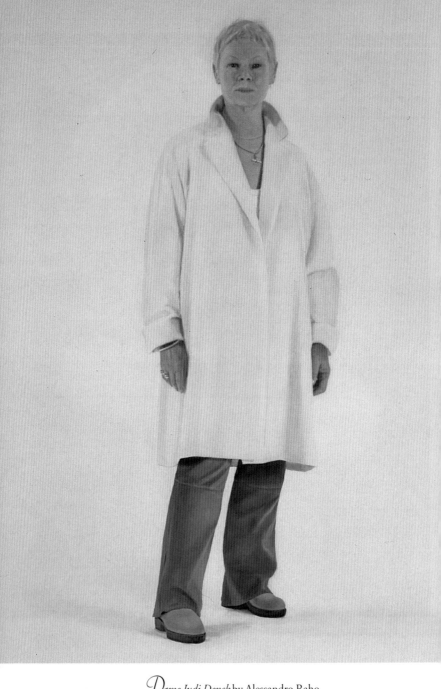

Dame Judi Dench by Alessandro Raho.

22/7   Our last break is over and we are back for the long final leg of the journey. I'll try from here forward to return to the daily record I have been keeping until the end of the run. Just to round things off in a complete way.

We were called at 2.15 for a sing-through and a warm-up. Jude was nursing a swollen hand as the result of being butted by a ram in Scotland. I will only add that it was the same hand that had previously been savaged by the mouse. We sang through the show, then worked voice with Patsy, followed by a movement class with Natalie. After the warm-up I was presented with a sensational cake in belated honour of my birthday. A stars and stripes cake, tastefully uncluttered with the dreaded fifty-seven candles.

23/7   Another very good show with a packed house. Our fear that we might go out with a whimper seems unjustified. Sean was in from the set of *Bent* which is in the final stages of shooting, first in Scotland and now in London. Peter and June Marychurch were back for a second go, and seemed to have really enjoyed themselves. We all met in Jude's room after, and Sean seemed to be pleased. Something he hardly ever expresses to us.

24/7   Two shows today. Exhausting as always. The matinée audience was classic. It was so dead that when Patricia said 'Plague' in the second act and there was absolutely no response from the front, the entire onstage company collapsed into giggles that lasted, it seemed, for the next twenty minutes. The evening audience much spiffier which really helps.

26/7   The show felt slightly below par tonight, and the audience was another tough one. Just like New York, as the run goes on the quality of the audiences seems to fall off.

Stephen Hanley is apparently home from the hospital, and not doing well. There is a feeling that the end might be coming. Brendan spent his time offstage taking comic photos of the cast for a photo montage card to send him.

Jude invited me down to her room after the performance to meet John Stride who was such a fine Romeo to her beautiful Juliet those many years ago.

2/8 I haven't written in a few days. The only news was the tragic death of Stephen Hanley. We were told he refused medical treatment except morphine, returned home and died a few days later. The recording of the show, which he so wanted to hear, was finally available shortly before he died. It accompanied his last hours and in that way we were all together one last time.

6/8 A difficult night of it, but we did good work. It really is amazing how consistent we are in this. The level of work maintained is very high. After a snoozy start the audience awoke to ovations at the end.

Another slip and a slide for Dame Jude in the Digs. This odd propensity for occasionally tipping over reminds me of her first entrance, I think it was in the technical, wearing an enormous hat. She slowly started to keel over, rather like Lucy in that showgirl episode. It was the first indication of a tendency to unexpected pratfalls that have hilariously plagued us throughout the year.

10/8 It was a tough day with the second show somewhat easier than the first. The back-stage event of the evening performance was a contest arranged for the company by Simon's dresser, Stephen. The contest was called 'Match that Dick', and involved trying to match the faces of several nude male models with photos of their willies. Despite a certain reluctance from some of the more dignified members of the company, everyone was shamed into participating. Tension runs high.

11/8 The winner was loudly announced over the back-stage intercom, 'Dame Judi Dench!' But no, stage management just jokin'. The winner was? Discretion dictates a tasteful withholding of the winner's name, lest publishing it should end his career.

14/8 Double whammy. There is trouble brewing over the cabaret the company is presenting after the final Friday night performance. Originally the idea was to repeat the successful evening of a few weeks ago. Unfortunately, Astrid caved, and now, as more and more people have decided to perform, the evening will be a very long one.

16/8 Things continue to fall apart around the cabaret. This is very unfortunate and is beginning to poison the end of the run. To make things even more difficult, recent audiences, although numerous, have not been too swift. Example. A woman came up to Jo Stewart as she was finishing up at the keyboard at the end of the performance, to ask the whereabouts of the harp. Jo explained that there was no harp in the band, but rather the sound was produced by the computerised keyboard she was playing. 'How extraordinary,' said the woman, 'it sounds so effective, especially in "Where are the crowds".'

19/8 The cabaret flap seems to have cooled. Hundreds of people will apparently perform. At least the world will have a chance to see 'Sixteen going on seventeen' once more!

There was a major scenic disaster at the top of the theatre scene. When the elevator rose to accompany the hanging flats to their upper position, the fly system, which is to raise the walls at the same speed as the elevator, failed to operate. As a result the flats collapsed and began to swing violently, crashing in all directions. It was a miracle nobody was crushed. The audience laughed merrily.

23/8 A note from Sean via Jude that we are underlining too heavily. So we did two very laid-back performances before two large and enthusiastic audiences. Home early as we are all invited to Jude and Michael's for a party tomorrow.

24/8 A wonderful day in inclement English summer weather. The food, company and setting were perfect. It was lovely for us all to be together before we finish. Lambert came over from France. Sean was there, the actors, their kids and other halves, and stage management. We had a fine time and were back in London about seven this evening.

30/8 Brendan and I took Jude for lunch to a terrific little restaurant called Live Bait. We had a fine time of it, and both gave her parting gifts, Brendan a mind-twisting game, and I the little bear I found, now with a ruff made from a bit of her Act Two petticoat.

Performance before a packed house, Sean present. It was apparently a success. After, we presented the long-suffering cabaret which was sold out and well received, but not so successful as it would have been in the short version, I venture to suggest. Tomorrow two shows, and the end of the trail.

31/8 The most moving and thrilling of last performances in my memory.

I went to work pushing all this-is-the-last-time-I-will-ever thoughts from my mind and aimed at doing the best two shows I could manage. The rest of the company seemed of the same mind. The matinée audience was a lovable one, attentive, warm and very appreciative. Many rose to their feet and cheered at the finish and we were all touched by the great affection they showed us.

The evening and final performance was on another scale altogether. Again, it was very difficult at first to keep concentrated, to let favourite moments go as they disappeared one after another into the past. The beginning of the Digs was particularly painful. Both our eyes filled with tears as we started, but we played well and truly together. When Jude opened her robe for 'the page that has been written on, and rewritten' she had emblazoned 'Go Home, Yank' on her corset. It was such a funny, dear thing to do that we sailed through the number and the rest of the scene, playing as well as ever we had done. There was huge and prolonged applause after 'You must meet my wife'. It stopped the show. The audience throughout remained exemplary, attentive, hugely responsive, but never destroying the flow. At the conclusion of the play pandemonium broke out. They literally stood and screamed for call after call. Finally the actors returned to their dressing rooms but the shouting continued. Jude and I were sent on for another call and the place went crazy. We came on again with the entire company now reassembled, and the ovation continued. Sondheim and Sean came up from the front of the house, more pandemonium, and much hugging and tears. Even Steve was weeping. Finally, after a couple more triumphant bows the evening and *A Little Night Music* came to rest.

I went to the party briefly, I wanted to see everyone but not really to stay. I made the rounds as quickly as possible and said good-bye to my friends, most sadly to my darling Jude. I grabbed a cab and went quickly home. Quite a night.

Under his Oxter

BILLY CONNOLLY

One of the nicer things about being tall is that you can measure yourself against the height above sea level of the Maldive Islands, which sit, apparently, some way off the coast of Sri Lanka. Personally, I measure exactly six feet in height. This places me in the international scale of well-known types as being taller than Douglas Bader (depending on which leg he is wearing that day), much taller than Albert Einstein, Toulouse-Lautrec, Napoleon and Judi Dench. The delightful thing about towering over Ms Dench is that when you are posing for photographs as John Brown standing with Dame Judi as Queen Victoria, you appear to be an immense agricultural Scottish person whose Queen's shoulder nestles neatly under his oxter (that's armpit to anyone who dwells south of North Berwick). Judi Dench, she of the Dame prefix, would seem to be the most popular person in the British Isles and possibly the entire empire since the death of the late Queen Mother. Judi also manages, between bouts of staggering popularity, to be an actor of galactic ability.

Her Dameship manages the impossible most days where she appears to take on the appearance of a delightful petite woman and a giant of the British Theatre who would appear to find situation comedy on television and acting in Shakespeare at Stratford-upon-Avon something of a dawdle (well within her grasp) and brings to both an appearance of familiarity and comfort that quite frankly takes the breath away from mere mortals like me, and anyone else who has had the luck to watch her in full flight. The only reason that I mention her height at all is because the moment that I think about her, or hear her name mentioned, I immediately recall how comfortable she is to hold, or stroll arm in arm with, or, to put it more picturesquely, to stroll shoulder to armpit with. The world's first completely compact and portable giant. Dame Judi Dench.

Our paths crossed in the most delightful of ways. I had been, or rather was, in the middle of making a television series about the history of Scottish art. We had travelled over great swathes of Europe from the Glasgow boys, the colourists who spent time outside Paris and learning from the French artists the nobility of the turnip and the onion when portrayed in oil on canvas, to the dwelling in Rome of the young pretender, Bonnie Prince Charlie, whose Roman domicile is now unfortunately a very ordinary bank whose management very graciously had the polystyrene tiles removed to expose the beautifully painted ceiling under-neath! Towards the end of filming I was standing on the hills above Holyrood Palace in Edinburgh talking to my producer, Douglas Rae, about the day's work, when he mentioned quite casually that he had got hold of the idea for a film about the story of the relationship between Queen Victoria and John Brown, the ghillie from Balmoral. I took immediate interest. I had heard in a giggly back of the hand manner since I was a schoolboy about the rough working-class man who had had an apparent love affair with the Queen. He asked me very casually, almost in the way that you would ask someone if they would like a cup of tea, if I would like to play the part of John Brown in the movie. I answered with something approximating 'My God, I'd love to', trying all the while to restrain myself from roly-polying down the hill to Holyrood Palace, screaming all the way.

When the dust settled and sanity prevailed, Douglas told me that the film was yet to be written, but that he had been shown tremendous interest in the project by some of the biggest names in British drama. My feelings went instantly from nervous fore-boding (my normal state) to abject fear and loss of will to live.

He mentioned that he was leaving the following day for London, when he would talk to Dame Judi and officially offer her the part of Queen Victoria. On a whim I said to him, 'Please, just for me, when you offer her the part, find a way in the conversation to drop in that she was not the first choice for the role and then go silent, or change the subject. If she is anything remotely like every actress I have ever met she will find it impossible not to ask you who the first choice happened to be. Appear loth to mention who it is, and do it as if you wanted to spare the feelings of the most unfortunate soul who, for her own reasons, couldn't do the part. On being pressed, cajoled, harried, nagged or, in the extremely unlikely event, physically attacked, release the information that the first choice was Bob Hoskins and tell me what effect it has.'

The reason I did this was that I was sure she would find it funny and perhaps put her in a silly way in touch with me, and secondly, because the first time I met Bob Hoskins was at the Edinburgh Festival some years before when he was dressed completely as Queen Victoria for a satirical role he was playing with the Ken Campbell road show. At the time he had told me about a fight he had been involved in, in a public toilet in Piccadilly Manchester while dressed as Queen Victoria, which can still make me laugh to this day, at least ten years on.

When Douglas sprang this information on Judi she apparently threw her head back and laughed peals of golden laughter in the way that only she can do. More about the laughter later.

The movie's screenplay was to be written by Jeremy Brock, and was waited for with bated breath. When it eventually arrived, it was greeted by all and sundry as no less than a masterpiece and had everyone leaping up and down with unbridled glee. Everyone, that is, except me. I immediately sank into a black depression, like a night-time free fall into a giant tin of boot polish. The very thought of acting with Judi had me terrified. I could see myself being exposed as an impostor, the drama equivalent of one of those grinning half-wits in a kilt sitting on a bale of hay in the Hogmanay show on television. At this point I came up with my master plan. I would have to meet her before it started. I asked Douglas to arrange a lunch for Judi and me in London. I couldn't face the idea that our first meeting would be at the read-through of the script where someone might giggle at my attempt to act with a living legend.

The request was met with furrowed brows and bewildered expressions, but none-the-less arranged, at the Caprice restaurant in St James's, a place where I felt comfortable. I arrived far too early and shuffled around in my seat, wondering what I would say to this woman, when I had an idea. I would nip out and buy myself a cigar that would settle my nerves a bit. Nervousness has invariably given me some really crap ideas. I set off for Dunhill's store, which was only one block away from the restaurant, and made my purchase. I was new to cigar-smoking then and it subsequently took longer than I expected because of all the well-meaning advice I was given by the manager of the store. It's hardly like buying a packet of fags. You never hear of cigarette-smokers sitting together talking about great fags they have smoked. In the event, it took ages more than I wanted it to and from my previous position of being early I was now late.

Cigars in pocket, I ran back to the restaurant to find Judi sitting at the table waiting for me. I apologised and went on at great length about the cigar store and why it took so long and was met with a warm tolerant smile that I would get to know and love very much in the following years, years of a friendship that I treasure in my heart, and shall for ever. During the lunch and the laughs that ensued I asked her if she would like to see my pierced nipples, of which I was very proud. I thought she would collapse on the spot. She turned down the opportunity in the giggling way that most people would turn down the idea of swimming the Channel in a duffel coat and wellies. We talked and laughed our way through lunch and found ourselves to be unified on several fronts. We like the same things and, more importantly, dislike the same things. I have always felt that most of my friends are my friends because of our dislike of the same things and dislike of the same people! Altogether the lunch went very well and we parted knowing each other a little better than we did before. For me, it turned out to be one of my better ideas. I was so much more relaxed than I had been before and I went off home with a big grin on my face.

The day of the read-through of the script arrived and we gathered, the entire cast, at a rather bleak room in that fancy new part of Chelsea down by the river where the docks used to be. Judi was her usual self, putting everyone at ease with her warm friendly manner. The reading went very well, I even felt so good that I sat beside Judi throughout. She was wonderful, and spread the feeling of warmth and confidence through the room. Judi has that indefinable quality of changing every room that she walks into; she seems to emanate a spirit of something very good, something very worthwhile. We had lunch where we talked and laughed with the cast of my dreams (Antony Sher, Geoffrey Palmer, Richard Pasco, David Westhead) and had the pleasure of hearing her laugh again. She has the female equivalent of the laugh of a docker, or maybe a blacksmith. It is a hearty, buxom, sexy laugh, which is adored, not only by comedians like me, but by everyone who has had the pleasure of being close to it.

The filming started soon after; our first scene together was one where I have been summoned to meet her in her summer-house on the Isle of Wight soon after my arrival with my horses. The scene was meant to be very tense, since she (the Queen) disapproved of John Brown's being there at all. It had been an idea of people in government to try to get her out of mourning the death of her husband, Prince Albert, and back into her duties as Queen which she hadn't been doing for a number of years. She was sitting at her desk with two ladies in waiting standing behind her and various lackeys dotted about the room when I was summoned to enter and be interviewed. I will never forget the power of the scene as long as I live. There was a long walk from the door to the desk, reminiscent of a court-martial entrance, which I tried to do in a semi-regimental manner with my kilt swinging around my milk-white legs. The Queen is busy reading her diary for a very long time and is eventually reminded that I am standing there waiting, when she looks up as the Queen and positively nails me to the floor with her expression of cold dissent. There is no going back now.

At the end of the meeting, after several enquiries by her about my family etc., I blurt out a statement to her about how much she must have loved her husband because she obviously missed him so much. Brown makes the comment very much as a new country fellow, which he indeed was. It has the most profound effect on her and she loses her temper in the most extraordinary way, bursting into tears and being escorted from the room in a dreadful emotional state, and I am roughly taken from the room, bewildered, having caused the entire scene. There and then I learned a salutary lesson. Actors of the quality of Judi Dench carry with them an ability to drag the very best from you. That is, when you are confronted by the power of talent so big there is no escape other than by acting right back again. There is no question of standing there waving your arms around and trying to remember the words; this is the real thing and it feels great.

Even in scenes where she wasn't present, like the times when I was standing outside the palace with my horse, refusing to leave my post against her wishes, I could feel her all around me, it was quite extraordinary. Her power to be, as opposed to, to act, would take my breath away sometimes when it was coming at me. There was a scene in a castle where we were attending a country dance. The music was wonderful as the fiddles took control of the eightsome reel and had us twirling around the floor with great energy and joy. At one point we were standing opposite one another in the ring of eight dancers when our eyes met and I saw her smile that lovely sensual smile of hers and thought, 'My God, Judi Dench fancies me, what am I to do?' Of course she didn't, but Queen Victoria didn't half fancy John Brown and it came screaming out to me, teaching me in no uncertain manner the difference between acting and 'being there'. Since the first scene in the room where I was interviewed and she burst into tears, I had become a different person, the penny had dropped. Especially when you consider that she did the scene ten or so times, bursting into tears in the most upsetting way every time. I felt like the most privileged man on earth.

It was also great to share in her sense of humour offstage where we shared many a laugh. I remember walking with her up the stairs of a castle down in the Scottish border country when we came upon the heads of some animals that had been shot by one of the previous toffs in some exotic part of the empire long ago. One of them was a sort of mountain goat with a white head and yellowish horns that curled from its head and in a thick swirl around its ears. As we neared it on the stairs Judi blurted out, 'Oh look, it's Michael Heseltine!' It was perfection.

When the film was finished we heard that it had been snatched up by the great film people Miramax and was to be released as a feature film all over the world. We were delighted, because it was originally intended for television to be broadcast in Britain by the BBC. Judi and I were sent over to America to do some publicity for it. We had the time of our lives trying not to take it too seriously while giving it the respect that it deserved. Most of the interviews were fine, if a little predictable, some of them pompous and unbearable, so we would resort to having a laugh. I would always be asked how it felt to act with Judi and would always answer that it was a nightmare, dealing with the long silences, the tantrums and the sudden mood swings. She would laugh, we both would laugh and life on the press junket would become bearable again.

People would even ask if she was serious all the time and had I learned anything from her? I always answered that the main thing I had learned was not to gamble with her. Several times during filming she would have a bet with me on when the shooting would finish that day. Normally the bet would be around fifty pounds. I didn't win even once. She would then go and buy me a present with her winnings, usually fishing flies or cigars.

The eventual success of the film, particularly in America, resulted in Judi being nominated for an Oscar. Every television set in Britain was tuned in to that event. Victory was not to be on that particular evening; she would have to wait for a year before striding beautifully off with the coveted award for her performance in *Shakespeare in Love*.

Despite the glittering prizes that come her way, she manages an occasional glance in my direction. We have remained friends of the closest gossiping giggling variety. Her visits to my house in Scotland, with husband Michael and daughter Finty, were looked forward to by the entire family. I still enjoy the eightsome reel with her on these occasions. I loved the company of Judi and Michael so much before he tragically passed away. I can still see them sitting on the green wicker chairs, Michael resplendent in his kilt with a shining amber glass in hand, listening to the music of the ceilidh in the woods in the glow of a bonfire. It took Judi a couple of years to return after Michael's death. When I saw her lovely face again it reminded me of Fyodor Dostoevsky's description of a woman in *The Brothers Karamazov*, 'a little tear, frozen in time'.

In recent years, when we dance the eightsome reel, I know she fancies me, and I would like the world to know that I fancy her right back. The mention of her name creates a lovely little party in my heart.

Re-inventing the Dame

DAVID HARE

Do young people in the regions now dream of the capital city with the same intensity with which we dreamed of London in the 1960s?

Forty years ago, as a schoolboy, my greatest wish was to get on the train from my small provincial town to see great actors in great plays. When I went to the Aldwych Theatre in 1961, I got my first sight of John Gielgud and of Peggy Ashcroft in *The Cherry Orchard*. Years later, I was told by the actors who appeared in it that it was not a very good production. John Gielgud had a flashy piece of business where Gaev was seen to be cheating at snooker. I didn't care if the production was good or not. My eyes were drawn to the young actress playing Anya, walking around, as I remember, in some kind of white dress, already at that age lit up from inside, speaking to each of us individually and all of us collectively – both at the same time. The figure of that seemingly frail girl has stayed with me throughout my theatre-going life. Once I wrote her a letter praising her work. She wrote back: 'You call me beautiful. You call me brilliant. I notice you don't call me tall.'

In the early eighties it was, typically, the British film director Stephen Frears who took Judi Dench out of the theatre and away from a slightly predictable line of classical parts to play a nurse in a television film called *Going Gently*. If Judi has a single problem, it is that she, like many great actors, very easily gets trapped behind the bars of the audience's expectation. More than

178

once, it has required an exceptional director to spring her from the impression of respectability that comes from doing what the audience requires of you. Stephen offered Judi the chance to leave Stratford and re-invent herself as the more interestingly contemporary actress she's now become. Two men were dying of cancer in beds, side by side. The emotion of the film was conveyed not by the death of the men, but by the nurse's response to it. The sight of Judi's expression as she folded linen onto the newly empty bed reminded you of the same lesson that Shakespeare's tragedies teach. It is not suffering which moves us. It is courage in the face of suffering.

If Frears was the first director to send Judi off in a radical direction – he remembers saying to her, 'Come and play with the boys from the wrong side of the tracks' – then John Madden was the second. When Madden cast Judi as Queen Victoria in *Mrs Brown* he managed to persuade you of the highly implausible proposition that royalty may be human beings as well. The film, clearly, has a powerful element of fiction. If, like me, you are not charmed by bonnet and blazer cinema, and even less by the grumpiness of the British monarchy itself, then the film is all the more remarkable. In that wonderful first thirty minutes, as Victoria grieves for her dead husband, Madden finds in Judi's face and in the desperate containment of her delivery a modernity and compassion which you could never have hoped for in so wooden a subject. It was more Bergman than Balmoral.

Once, making a film with Judi in Bangkok, I was standing at the side of the set while the director revised a particularly elaborate camera movement. Judi beckoned me over and asked me, 'What do I mean here when I say "yes"?' I replied, 'You mean "no".' At once Judi jumped in, frightened that I might insult her intelligence. 'Fine. Don't say any more.' On the next take, she delivered the line 'Yes' perfectly to mean 'No.' It was then I realised that Judi's gift is grounded in unusual technical freedom. With many actors you struggle towards one performance. Judi offers you the possibility of many. She may at times be nervous.

All her favourite stories are about disaster and mishap onstage; get her to tell you the story about Gloucester's eye in *King Lear* being gouged out over-vigorously, so that the vile jelly flew past her right shoulder and adhered to the wall of the set. But, at bottom, she is not frightened. She is not frightened because she is free.

I did once observe that acting is a judgment on character. It is the remark of mine which has been most often repeated back to me. I would like a royalty for every time I have seen it quoted in print. When I made the remark, I was thinking of how the years go by and of how, as you get older as an actor, the question of who you are may become just as important as who you are pretending to be. We only have to think of Paul Newman, of Jason Robards, of John Gielgud himself to know that the audience responds not just to the pretence, but to the accumulation of wisdom and experience behind the pretence. They look at Judi and like what they see. They trust who she is.

It is superfluous for me to pay tribute to Judi Dench. No tribute can match the tribute she has paid me by appearing in my play, *Amy's View*. Nearly forty years on, the provincial boy lives in Hampstead, a famously literary leafy suburb of London. Peggy Ashcroft lived a few hundred yards away. Only a graveyard separates my house from Judi Dench's. My own journey is only one of ten thousand made by fellow professionals who have used Judi as a means of navigation. No doubt, even now, a younger director or writer is waiting in some small town one day to reveal aspects of Judi Dench so far hidden.

This is the text of a speech given in 1999 at the Barrymore Theater in New York when Judi Dench was awarded The Golden Quill by The Shakespeare Guild.

Dench-olatry

GREGORY DORAN

One Tuesday afternoon in May 2003 I dropped Judi Dench a postcard, asking her if she'd consider playing the Countess of Rossillion in *All's Well That Ends Well* which I would be directing for the Royal Shakespeare Company in the Swan Theatre in Stratford-upon-Avon that autumn. The following morning I got a phone call. It was Judi. 'The Countess? *All's Well?* The Swan? This autumn? Yes, to all four questions,' she said.

Well, it never happens like that. As a director, you can woo actors for years in advance to play a certain part or come and do a season in Stratford and then what often happens is that they get a film or a juicy telly right at the last minute, and you are left desperately flicking through *Spotlight*, the actors' directory, for inspiration.

I've admired Judi Dench for years. Of course, who hasn't? My Dench-olatry began in the early seventies when I would hitch-hike down from Preston with my school mate Richard Sharples, and camp on Stratford racecourse, getting up bright and early to queue for day tickets or returns at the theatre. We saw her as Beatrice in John Barton's glorious Raj *Much Ado About Nothing*, with Donald Sinden as Benedick, as Regan in *King Lear*, and a great highlight was managing to get seats to see Trevor Nunn and Guy Woolfenden's delightful musical version of *The Comedy of Errors*, set in a bustling Mediterranean market square.

Seated on the special audience gallery – actually on the stage –

among the tarts and the washing, we got to see all the company in close-up: Michael Williams, Roger Rees, Nickolas Grace and all; and the sublime moment when Judi, as the frustrated wife Adriana, emerged onto the balcony, stabbed her finger at the man she supposed was her tardy husband, pointed back to the house where his supper was waiting, and then flounced back inside, without a word. A wonderful comic moment, rooted in the reality of that woman's anger, seething and slightly sozzled.

Later at the Young Vic, and by now a drama student, I saw Judi as Lady Macbeth, and realised that she could bring that same ruthlessly truthful instinct to tragedy with powerful effect. The moment when Lady Macbeth summons up the spirits that tend on mortal thoughts, Judi suddenly recoiled, terrified at what she might be daring to unleash. And like most great moments of theatre it was so simple; honest and simple.

Judi's last appearance with the RSC in Stratford had been as Imogen in *Cymbeline*, in 1979, and although she had appeared with the company at the Barbican, as Mother Courage in 1984, and in Peter Shaffer's *The Gift of the Gorgon* in 1992, *All's Well* would mark her first return to Stratford in twenty-four years. It was going to be a major event!

'I don't know the play,' she said. 'Never seen it, read it, or been in it. You're going to have to tell me the story.' A few days later, I found myself walking around Judi's beautiful garden in Surrey telling her the story of the play with its fiendishly complicated ring plot, which I'm quite sure I messed up completely. Sammy, her six-year-old grandson, flitted in and out of the trees, looking for all the fairy kingdom like Puck overhearing our conference.

I told her of my growing theory that perhaps the particular elegiac tone of this bittersweet play suggested that there was something autobiographical about it, and that parallels between the Countess of Rossillion and Mary, Countess of Pembroke, might prove revealing. After all, we know Shakespeare had been at Wilton, the Pembrokes' family home, in 1603, just months before he wrote the play, and that the recently widowed Countess had written to her headstrong son, William Herbert, to join them there.

Not that any of that would necessarily help her play the part. Although of course the fact that Judi, like the Countess, had recently had to cope with the loss of her husband, Michael Williams, would mean she would have a profound understanding of her pain. But that was, I suspected, too raw and too personal for me to approach, and we never talked about that aspect of the Countess until the very last moment of the rehearsals.

As I left, she said she had a good feeling about the whole thing, and that we would talk.

I suspect there were a few anxious moments before she phoned again to confirm, a couple of weeks later. Coming back to Stratford after all this time, where she had lived with Michael and the family and had such a happy time, where there were so many ghosts and so many memories, must have been a hard decision to make.

'Well, the answer's Yes,' she said, 'but you've got Finty to thank.' Apparently her daughter, Finty, had finally persuaded her to do it, arguing that she had spent so much of her happy childhood in Stratford and she wanted her son Sammy to have something of the same experience.

The news spread like wildfire around Stratford. The girls in the Box Office and the Wardrobe, the back-stage crew, dressers, and front-of-house staff, folk at the Shakespeare Institute, and even at the Dirty Duck would stop me to check that the rumours were true. By the time I saw Judi again the deal was signed and sealed. Ten weeks in Stratford over Christmas, and then a transfer into the Gielgud Theatre in the West End in February for another ten.

Judi came up to the Swan to do a recital with Ian Richardson for the annual Stratford poetry festival in June. It gave her a chance to check out the theatre, and gave me the opportunity to watch her demonstrate once again her quite extraordinary ability to get inside someone else's skin; on this occasion a little girl at a party in a story called 'The Thrush and the Jay' by Sylvia Lynd.

In the story the child is sitting at the party table waiting for the cake to be passed around, only to find that when it comes to her it's nearly all gone. Someone else might have sent up the story for laughs, not Judi. The girl's outrage at the injustice, her suppressed fury, her bitter struggle to hold back her tears, were so real, so recognisable and of course, as a result, hilarious.

Talking about the Swan after the recital, Judi said that she had suddenly remembered a moment during the rehearsals for *The Comedy of Errors* in 1976 (which were held in what was known as the Conference Hall, and is now the Swan Theatre). 'We were rehearsing that funny business with the intercom, do you remember? And Mikey [Michael Williams] was up a ladder and he suddenly looked round the room and said to Trevor, "This place would make a bloody good theatre!"' Apparently Trevor had gone very quiet. Clearly plans were already in hand to convert the space.

We began rehearsals for *All's Well* in October, in Clapham at St Peter's Hall, often affectionately referred to as St Peter Hall. Judi was finishing a film for the first week, so she missed the initial work of reading the play and taking the text apart line by line. But I deliberately waited to do any full reading of the play or any model showing until her arrival.

On the Monday morning of the second week, I arrived at St Peter's awash with nerves. She arrived with a streaming cold. She put her bag down by the door, a ritual I had heard about. She never quite believes the part is meant to be hers, so she leaves her bag by the door in case a hasty exit is required. I have a rule that if anyone's mobile phone goes off in rehearsal, they are charged five pounds (and twenty-five pounds if it goes off during a run, which I'm glad to say has never happened). Within moments of her arrival, in her bag, Judi's phone went off. We knew immediately that it was hers from the ring tone: the James Bond theme tune.

Ice broken, we got on with the serious business of rehearsal;

although I suspect laughter is never very far away when Judi Dench rehearses. In the first scene, Bertram enquires: 'What is it, my good lord, the king languishes of?' and the Lord Lafeu replies laconically, 'A fistula, my lord.' For some reason, it took about a week for Judi and fellow culprits Charles Kay and Jamie Glover (playing Lafeu and Bertram) to get past the word 'fistula'.

The role of the Countess is relatively small, but she's the beating heart of the play. When Trevor Nunn attracted Peggy Ashcroft to play the part in his beautiful Chekhovian 1981 production, he had identified the vital need for the audience to care for the Countess. He had wanted to open the Swan Theatre with *All's Well*, convinced that it was a Blackfriars play, requiring the intimacy of a smaller house, but the project to build the Swan had been delayed and he had to mount the production in the main house.

Attracting actresses of the calibre of Judi Dench or Peggy Ashcroft to play the Countess has a considerable precedent, as Edith Evans, Celia Johnson, Barbara Jefford and Flora Robson have all played the part. George Bernard Shaw, giving a coruscating review to a production of *All's Well* by a non-commercial group called the Irving Dramatic Club in 1895, castigated the actress playing the Countess for being unable to discover any of her 'wonderfully pleasant good sense, humanity and originality'. It was, he said, 'the most beautiful old woman's part ever written'.

Now, as the occasion for this book somewhat ungallantly reminds us, Judi has reached the three score years and ten, a fact that seems impossible to believe in her company; and no one would describe her as 'old'. In fact I think I omitted the word from Shaw's description when I recounted it to her (or perhaps I softened it to 'older'). However, the character makes several references to her age, a fact which taxed Judi.

'She keeps on going on about her age,' she would say. '"My heart is heavy and my age is weak", or she says she rejoices that she'll see the king before she dies. Is she about to pop her clogs? How old am I meant to play her?'

I said I thought the accumulated burden of grief, at the loss of her husband, and now her son, at the troubles he gets himself into and the abandonment of Helena, all that makes the Countess feel her age weighing upon her.

'So how old am I meant to play her?'

I urged Judi to play herself, at which she roared, 'Oh, thank you very much! My director thinks I'm decrepit!'

Throughout rehearsals Judi continued to explore and deepen the Countess's relationship with her clown, and with her surrogate daughter Helena. She'd often surprise us with sudden flashes of feeling in the Countess, for instance at the point where the Dumaine brothers bring the news that her son has gone to war, she turned on them in a sudden blistering fury when they attempt to excuse his actions. She'd work tirelessly at focusing and refining the laughs, delighting in the invention of giving the clown Lavache (Mark Lambert) a bath, but she was as rigorous at ensuring that every moment of the last scene, as revelation follows revelation, was given its proper shock weight and emotional significance.

The younger actors would often sit in on rehearsals with Judi. To listen to her deliver the text was to hear a master class in Shakespeare's verse. She would feel the verse line, beating out the iambic rhythm on her hand if in doubt where the stress lay. And in early stages she would not be able to remember the line if the pulse was wrong. She'd seek to release the easy natural effects of the line endings, never pausing so much as lifting and considering the end of a line before completing the sense with the next. For example, when the Countess (in Act One, Scene Three) says to Helena as she dissembles her love for Bertram:

> *My fear hath catch'd your fondness; now I see*
> *The mystery of your loneliness, and find*
> *Your salt tears' head. Now to all sense 'tis gross:*
> *You love my son . . .*

at the end of the first line, where others may have run on, Judi would lift the word 'see', allowing the next phrase ('the mystery of your loneliness') to be considered precisely, and compassionately expressed. And lifting the end of the second line allowed her to land on the next four monosyllables with tough maternal love, leading on to the revelation that she wants to flush out of Helena: 'You love my son.'

If that sounds all very technical it's because it is. Classical acting wouldn't be a craft if there weren't disciplines involved. The art is to hide the technique, to marry application with inspiration, and balance concentration with relaxation. Like a great master craftsman, Judi not only continues to hone her craft, but passes it on.

Press night. Usually on a first night you don't want to rehearse the actors during the day. They don't need new things to think about at this performance, and anyway they are busy writing cards for the company, or leaving keys for guests coming up to stay. On the other hand it's important to come together to focus and to do some work together, some voice perhaps, and some relaxation exercises maybe.

At the end of the afternoon, I always take the company upstairs into the Swan Gallery to have a look at the Flowers portrait of Shakespeare which the RSC owns, and at some of the memorabilia from past productions. This year there is an exhibition about the two Shakespeare plays in the winter season, *All's Well* and *Othello*, which I am also directing, with my partner Tony Sher as Iago. They have mounted displays of costumes worn by Judi and Tony in past productions.

In Judi's cabinet there is her costume as Isabella in *Measure for Measure*, and as Beatrice and Adriana, though she is convinced that the costume marked Viola is not the same colour as the doublet she wore in the role. Her Lady Macbeth costume isn't on display. By a strange coincidence, Claudie Blakley is wearing that very dress as Helena in her disguise as a pilgrim. A neat handing on of tradition.

And that, I suppose, is why I always bring companies here, so that they can claim their right to do these plays, to realise that they are now the RSC and to assume the mantle. The RSC isn't just where it's been, but where it's going as well.

As we dispersed, Judi grabbed me. 'Just do something for me, Greg, if you can,' she said. 'Just put into a few words for me what makes this woman particular. Who is she? Not now, don't tell me now, but if you can think of what that is, pop into my dressing room and let me know. Only if you've time.'

I hurried on with the business of delivering the last few notes to actors, checking a few stage management queries, and ensuring that the creative team were all happy and, perhaps half an hour later, I popped into her room.

'I think it's this,' I said, trying to distil what we had learned over the journey of the last few weeks about the Countess. 'I think she is struggling to get over the loss of her husband, and now deal with the loss of her son too. And that's painful. There are distractions, like Lavache, but the pain won't go away.'

'Yes,' she said quietly, 'well, I know about that.'

When the Countess discovers that Helena loves Bertram, she realises that she's gaining a daughter, and pours all her efforts and love into her young ward. That makes the loss of Helena in the middle of the play almost intolerable for her, and why her eventual recovery in Act Five can't be expressed in words.

I think all I was describing was what Judi was already doing; she just wanted confirmation.

The Countess says nothing when Helena returns, as if from the dead, at the end of the play. Her new daughter-in-law turns to the Countess with the line, 'Oh, my dear mother, do I see you living?' There is no reply. There can't be. Judi's choice was for the Countess to stare at Helena, almost unable to move, and finally, slowly turn her outstretched hands palm up to signal silent welcome, acceptance, and profound relief. It was a moment to haunt you with its stillness, and she created it with such economy and truth, the effect was devastating.

Dench-olatry

I can watch what Judi Dench does, study it, admire it, comment on it, but I can't tell you how she does it; how she makes silence eloquent or humanity palpable. It's just her. It's why she's great.

Postscript

JOHN MILLER

*O*f Judi ever seriously thought that there was the slightest possibility of her seventieth birthday going unnoticed, she was to be massively disabused as 9 December 2004 approached.

On the Sunday beforehand she headed a stellar cast in a fund-raising gala for Peter Hall's new Rose Theatre at Kingston in Surrey (modelled on the original ground-plan for Shakespeare's Rose), which Peter asked me to produce, having already booked Judi to appear in it. The evening was billed as *Judi Dench and Friends*, several of whom arrived with large and fragile boxes which were deposited in her dressing-room. Judi also seized the opportunity of returning the famous black glove to Tim Pigott-Smith, by having him called to the stage and then hurling it at his feet from the gallery. Tim grinned and bowed in acknowledgment, saying, 'So it continues!'

Two days later my BBC Birthday Tribute was broadcast on Radio 2. I had not expected Judi to hear it on transmission, knowing she never watches herself on television, so I was both touched and surprised when she rang me immediately it ended to thank me.

On the day itself the press went to town. The *Daily Express* asked me to write a two-page spread to mark the occasion, Michael Coveney did the same in the *Independent*, and most of the rest ran pictures and stories. Judi herself was working, on one of the last days of shooting for *Mrs Henderson Presents*, Stephen Frears's film about the woman who bought the Windmill Theatre.

So most of the customary birthday celebrations had to be post-poned, including the long-planned presentation to her of a spe-cially bound copy of the hardback edition of this book. The earliest date we could find in her diary was not until 20 January 2005, when my publisher Ion Trewin hosted a lunchtime party at the Garrick Club, attended by as many of the contributors as we could gather, and we all inscribed it for her. In her short but heartfelt speech of thanks, Judi said with a rueful chuckle, 'This has to have been the longest birthday celebration ever, and now I think it must stop.'

In addition to the various lunches, dinners and parties given by her many devoted friends, only two days previously she had unveiled the new portrait of her by Alessandro Raho at the National Portrait Gallery, which has been added to the illus-trations in this edition of *Darling Judi*. She looked more than a touch apprehensive as she waited for the picture to be revealed, at which point we all moved in for a closer look. Judi was standing next to Trevor Nunn, and I couldn't resist asking him, 'Isn't that rather how Judi looks at the director when she says "Do you really want me to do that?"' Trevor's response was much more gallant, as he murmured 'Age cannot wither her, nor custom stale her infinite variety.' This Cleopatra just giggled at both of us, and then admitted how nervous she had been at the prospect of seeing herself represented on this lifesize canvas. The artist was so anxious not to detract from the overall effect by putting an obtrusive signature on to the all-white background that he signed it on the top edge of the frame, way out of sight.

Happily, there seems little risk of the lady herself disappearing from our sight. Discussions are under way for several film pro-jects, and for her return to the stage in early 2005. She has also been pressing me for some time to complete the script of a new comic recital for her, *Great Eccentrics*, which should have been revealed to the public before this edition rolls off the presses.

At the end of the Radio 2 broadcast Ian McKellen expressed a birthday wish that was also an appeal: 'Please Judi, don't build a new garden or a house or some project that the rest of us can't really enjoy, keep on doing what you've done so wonderfully well; because one of the great joys of being alive now is to be alive at the time that Judi Dench is here, and the thought that she might be sitting at home quietly just won't do.'

And so say all of us.

Chronology of Parts

Date	Play	Role	Theatre
1957	York Mystery Plays	Virgin Mary	St Mary's Abbey
The Old Vic Company, 1957–61			
1957	*Hamlet*	Ophelia	Old Vic
	Measure for Measure	Juliet	Old Vic
	A Midsummer Night's Dream	First Fairy	Old Vic
1958	*Twelfth Night*	Maria	Old Vic
	Henry V (Both plays also on tour to North America)	Katharine	Old Vic
1959	*The Double Dealer*	Cynthia	Old Vic
	As You Like It	Phebe	Old Vic
	The Importance of Being Earnest	Cecily	Old Vic
	The Merry Wives of Windsor	Anne Page	Old Vic
1960	*Richard II*	Queen	Old Vic
	Romeo and Juliet (Also Venice Festival)	Juliet	Old Vic
	She Stoops to Conquer	Kate Hardcastle	Old Vic
	A Midsummer Night's Dream (And walk-ons in *King Lear* and *Henry VI*)	Hermia	Old Vic

Date	Play	Role	Theatre
	The Royal Shakespeare Company, 1961–2		
1961	*The Cherry Orchard*	Anya	Aldwych
1962	*Measure for Measure*	Isabella	Stratford
	A Midsummer Night's Dream	Titania	Stratford
	A Penny for a Song	Dorcas Bellboys	Aldwych
	The Nottingham Playhouse Company, 1963		
1963	*Macbeth*	Lady Macbeth	Nottingham
	Twelfth Night (Both plays also on tour to West Africa)	Viola	Nottingham
	A Shot in the Dark	Josefa Lautenay	Lyric
	The Oxford Playhouse Company, 1964–5		
1964	*Three Sisters*	Irina	Oxford
	The Twelfth Hour	Anna	Oxford
1965	*The Alchemist*	Dol Common	Oxford
	Romeo and Jeannette	Jeannette	Oxford
	The Firescreen	Jacqueline	Oxford
	The Nottingham Playhouse Company, 1965–6		
1965	*Measure for Measure*	Isabella	Nottingham
	Private Lives	Amanda	Nottingham
1966	*The Country Wife*	Margery Pinchwife	Nottingham
	The Astrakhan Coat	Barbara	Nottingham
	St Joan	Joan	Nottingham

Chronology of Parts

Date	Play	Role	Theatre
The Oxford Playhouse Company, 1966–7			
1966	*The Promise*	Lika	Oxford
	The Rules of the Game	Silia	Oxford
1967	*The Promise*	Lika	Fortune
1968	*Cabaret*	Sally Bowles	Palace
The Royal Shakespeare Company, 1969–71			
1969	*The Winter's Tale*	Hermione/Perdita	Stratford
	Women Beware Women	Bianca	Stratford
	Twelfth Night	Viola	Stratford
1970	*London Assurance*	Grace Harkaway	Aldwych
	Major Barbara	Barbara Undershaft	Aldwych
1971	*The Merchant of Venice*	Portia	Stratford
	The Duchess of Malfi	Duchess	Stratford
	Toad of Toad Hall	Fieldmouse, Stoat and Mother Rabbit	Stratford
1973	*Content to Whisper*	Aurelia	Royal, York
	The Wolf	Vilma	Playhouse, Oxford
	(Also at Apollo, Queen's & New London)		
1974	*The Good Companions*	Miss Trant	Her Majesty's
1975	*The Gay Lord Quex*	Sophy Fullgarney	Albery
The Royal Shakespeare Company, 1975–80			
1975	*Too True to be Good*	Sweetie Simpkins	Aldwych

Chronology of Parts

Date	Play	Role	Theatre
1976	*Much Ado About Nothing*	Beatrice	Stratford
	Macbeth (Also Donmar and Young Vic)	Lady Macbeth	Stratford
	The Comedy of Errors	Adriana	Stratford
	King Lear	Regan	Stratford
1977	*Pillars of the Community*	Lona Hessel	Aldwych
1978	*The Way of the World*	Millamant	Aldwych
1979	*Cymbeline*	Imogen	Stratford
1980	*Juno and the Paycock*	Juno Boyle	Aldwych
1981	*A Village Wooing*	Young woman	New End

The National Theatre Company, 1982

Date	Play	Role	Theatre
1982	*The Importance of Being Earnest*	Lady Bracknell	Lyttelton
	A Kind of Alaska	Deborah	Cottesloe
1983	*Pack of Lies*	Barbara Jackson	Lyric

The Royal Shakespeare Company, 1984–5

Date	Play	Role	Theatre
1984	*Mother Courage*	Mother Courage	Barbican
1985	*Waste*	Amy O'Connell	Barbican and Lyric
1986	*Mr and Mrs Nobody*	Carrie Pooter	Garrick

The National Theatre Company, 1987–9

Date	Play	Role	Theatre
1987	*Antony and Cleopatra*	Cleopatra	Olivier
	Entertaining Strangers	Sarah Eldridge	Cottesloe
1989	*Hamlet*	Gertrude	Olivier

Chronology of Parts

Date	Play	Role	Theatre
1989	*The Cherry Orchard*	Ranevskaya	Aldwych
1991	*The Plough and the Stars*	Bessie Burgess	Young Vic
The National Theatre Company, 1991			
1991	*The Sea*	Mrs Rafi	Lyttelton
1992	*Coriolanus*	Volumnia	Chichester
The Royal Shakespeare Company, 1992			
1992	*The Gift of the Gorgon*	Helen Damson	Barbican and Wyndham's
The National Theatre Company, 1994–8			
1994	*The Seagull*	Arkadina	Olivier
1995	*Absolute Hell*	Christine Foskett	Lyttelton
	A Little Night Music	Desirée Armfeldt	Olivier
1997	*Amy's View*	Esmé	Lyttelton
1998	*Amy's View*	Esmé	Aldwych
	Filumena	Filumena	Piccadilly
1999	*Amy's View*	Esmé	Barrymore, New York
2001	*The Royal Family*	Fanny Cavendish	Theatre Royal, Haymarket
2002	*The Breath of Life*	Frances	Theatre Royal, Haymarket
2003	*All's Well That Ends Well*	The Countess	Swan, Stratford-upon-Avon, and Gielgud

DIRECTOR

Date	Title	Companies/Venues
1988	*Much Ado About Nothing*	Renaissance Theatre Company
1989	*Look Back in Anger*	Renaissance Theatre Company
	Macbeth	Central School of Speech and Drama
1991	*The Boys from Syracuse*	Regent's Park Open Air Theatre
1993	*Romeo and Juliet*	Regent's Park Open Air Theatre

TELEVISION

Date	Title	Company
1959	*Family on Trial*	Associated-Rediffusion
1960	*Z-Cars*	BBC
1960	*Henry V – Age of Kings*	BBC
1962	*Major Barbara*	BBC
1963	*The Funambulists*	ATV
1965	*Safety Man – Mogul*	BBC
1966	*Talking to a Stranger*	BBC
1968	*On Approval*	Yorkshire
1970	*Confession – Neighbours*	Granada
1972	*Luther*	BBC
1973	*Keep an Eye on Amelie*	BBC
1977	*The Comedy of Errors* (RSC)	Thames
1978	*Macbeth* (RSC)	Thames
1978	*Langrishe Go Down*	BBC

Chronology of Parts

Date	Title	Company
1978	*A Village Wooing*	Yorkshire
1979	*On Giant's Shoulders*	BBC
1979	*Love in a Cold Climate*	Thames
1980–3	*A Fine Romance*	London Weekend
1980	*The Cherry Orchard*	BBC
1980	*Going Gently*	BBC
1982	*Saigon – Year of the Cat*	Thames
1985	*The Browning Version*	BBC
1985	*Mr & Mrs Edgehill*	BBC
1985	*Ghosts*	BBC
1986	*Make and Break*	BBC
1988	*Behaving Badly*	Channel 4
1990	*Can You Hear Me Thinking?*	BBC
1990	*The Torch*	BBC
1991	*Absolute Hell*	BBC
1991–2002	*As Time Goes By*	BBC
1999	*The Last of the Blonde Bombshells*	BBC

FILMS

Date	Title	Director
1964	*The Third Secret*	Charles Crichton
1965	*He Who Rides a Tiger*	Charles Crichton
1965	*A Study in Terror*	James Hill

Chronology of Parts

Date	Title	Director
1965	*Four in the Morning*	Anthony Simmons
1965	*A Midsummer Night's Dream*	Peter Hall
1973	*Dead Cert*	Tony Richardson
1984	*Wetherby*	David Hare
1985	*A Room with a View*	James Ivory
1986	*84 Charing Cross Road*	David Jones
1987	*A Handful of Dust*	Charles Sturridge
1988	*Henry V*	Kenneth Branagh
1994	*Jack and Sarah*	Tim Sullivan
1995	*Goldeneye*	Martin Campbell
1995	*Hamlet*	Kenneth Branagh
1996	*Mrs Brown*	John Madden
1997	*Tomorrow Never Dies*	Roger Spottiswoode
1998	*Shakespeare in Love*	John Madden
1999	*Tea with Mussolini*	Franco Zeffirelli
1999	*The World is Not Enough*	Michael Apted
2000	*Chocolat*	Lasse Hallström
2001	*The Shipping News*	Lasse Hallström
2001	*Iris*	Richard Eyre
2001	*The Importance of Being Earnest*	Oliver Parker
2002	*Die Another Day*	Lee Tamahori
2004	*Ladies in Lavender*	Charles Dance
2004	*The Chronicles of Riddick*	Vin Diesel

A Note on the Contributors

JOHN MILLER wrote the authorised biography *Judi Dench: with a crack in her voice.*

BENEDICT NIGHTINGALE is the theatre critic for *The Times.*

BARBARA LEIGH-HUNT has appeared with Judi at the Old Vic, the RSC and in the West End.

IAN RICHARDSON was a member of the RSC with Judi in the 1960s and has accompanied her in poetry recitals since.

RICHARD EYRE directed Judi in *The Cherry Orchard* on BBC TV, *Amy's View* at the National Theatre and in the film of *Iris.*

STANLEY WELLS has made a particular study of Judi's Shakespearean performances, from the RSC to the National Theatre.

MICHAEL PENNINGTON has appeared opposite Judi at the RSC and in the West End.

TREVOR NUNN directed Judi in her award-winning performances as Lady Macbeth and Juno, and in many other productions for the RSC.

BOB LARBEY wrote the TV sitcoms *A Fine Romance* and *As Time Goes By.*

BILL NIGHY appeared opposite Judi in *Absolute Hell* on BBC TV, and *The Seagull* at the National Theatre.

DEARBHLA MOLLOY acted with Judi in Sean O'Casey's *Juno and the Paycock* and *The Plough and the Stars.*

HUGH WHITEMORE wrote *Pack of Lies* and the screenplay for *84 Charing Cross Road.*

MARTIN JARVIS played Jack Worthing to Judi's Lady Bracknell in *The Importance of Being Earnest* at the National Theatre and has appeared with her in several television productions.

A Note on the Contributors

TIM PIGOTT-SMITH appeared with Judi in *Antony and Cleopatra* and *Entertaining Strangers* at the National Theatre.

NED SHERRIN directed Judi in *Mr and Mrs Nobody*.

LAURENCE GUITTARD played opposite Judi in *A Little Night Music* at the National Theatre.

BILLY CONNOLLY played John Brown to Judi's Queen Victoria in *Mrs Brown*.

DAVID HARE wrote the script for *Saigon: Year of the Cat* on Thames Television, *Amy's View* for the National Theatre, and *The Breath of Life* at the Theatre Royal, Haymarket.

GREGORY DORAN directed *All's Well That Ends Well* which marked Judi's return to the RSC in 2003 after a twenty-year gap.

Index

Index

Index

Index

Index

Index

Index